H. NORMAN WRIGHT

ONE MARRIAGE UNDER GOD

Multnomah Publishers® *Sisters, Oregon*

ONE MARRIAGE UNDER GOD
published by Multnomah Publishers, Inc.

© 2005 by H. Norman Wright
International Standard Book Number: 1-59052-484-5

Cover design by The DesignWorks Group, Inc.
Cover image by Stephen Gardner, PixelWorksStudio.net
Interior design and typeset by Katherine Lloyd, The DESK

Unless otherwise indicated, Scripture quotations are from:
The Holy Bible, New International Version © 1973, 1984 by International
Bible Society, used by permission of Zondervan Publishing House.

Other Scripture quotations are from:
The Holy Bible, New Century Version (NCV) © 1987, 1988, 1991
by Word Publishing. Used by permission.
The Message © 1993, 1994, 1995, 1996, 2000, 2001, 2002.
Used by permission of NavPress Publishing Group.

Multnomah is a trademark of Multnomah Publishers, Inc.,
and is registered in the U.S. Patent and Trademark Office.
The colophon is a trademark of Multnomah Publishers, Inc.

Printed in the United States of America

For information:
MULTNOMAH PUBLISHERS, INC.
601 N. LARCH ST. • SISTERS, OREGON 97759

Library of Congress Cataloging-in-Publication Data
Wright, H. Norman.
One marriage under God / H. Norman Wright.
    p. cm.
ISBN 1-59052-484-5
1. Marriage--Religious aspects--Christianity. I. Title.
BV835.W7445 2005
248.4--dc22
                                          2005011924

05 06 07 08 09 10—10 9 8 7 6 5 4 3 2 1 0

CONTENTS

Chapter One

BREAKING
THE SILENCE

YOUR PHONE RINGS. It's one of your closest friends. You hear the words "It's over"…and then silence. Then the words begin to tumble out: "I haven't been happy in this marriage for years. Why stay and be miserable? Nothing seems to make a change! We're all miserable, so at least divorce will give both of us a fresh start and a chance at finding a soul mate. And the kids are resilient. They can adjust. I just need some people in my corner to support me right now."

True, the cry of a person who feels trapped in a marriage is a daily occurrence. But it's a different scenario when you hear this from a *friend*. What can you say? What *would* you say to your friend at this time? Think about it.

You're in a restaurant and you see a young couple from church. At one time you were this young woman's Sunday school teacher. She introduces you to her friend John and says, "We're so excited! We just moved in together. Someday we may want to get married, but we want to make sure we're compatible and that we really love each other. Marriage is so risky and so many people get divorced. This way we can finish our education without all the pressures and financial problems of marriage. So what do you think?"

What can you say to that? What *would* you say?

Rest assured that marriage as we know it hasn't ended. It never will. Oh, it's taken some hits. It's been assaulted on several fronts with a vengeance. Many would like to expand its meaning and definition in our society. But these attacks have been occurring for years, often with a subtlety that hides the erosion that has occurred.

David Gushee gave a vivid description in his book *Getting Marriage Right*. He likened marriage to a cathedral that is in the state of collapse—its foundation and supports have been in a state of gradual erosion for generations and we are only now experiencing the result.[1]

Our culture is not only indifferent to marriage, but a bit hostile. It's no longer "in" to say marriage is a better way; the alternatives are considered to be more attractive.

Houston, we have a problem.

Only now the problem is not a glitch in space but an attack on the very foundation of the traditional family. Just a few of the trends that have been moving in a negative direction: first-time marrieds, children born to married mothers, children living with both mom and dad. Meanwhile, never-marrieds, cohabitation, and children born to and living with

ONE MARRIAGE UNDER GOD

unmarried mothers are on the rise. Look closely. You'll see these affecting your own community and church.

And so we exclaim, "God, we have a problem." He already knows. The question is whether *we* know how serious it is. And are we willing to engage our divorce-friendly culture in a direct confrontation?

It's not just couples who divorce who have given up and quit on God's plan for marriage. The rest of us contribute to the problem when we remain silent while marriages around us disintegrate. When two people stand before witnesses and the church and pledge themselves to one another until parted by death, there is no "quit clause" in the contract. This is too often inserted later.

Marriage is a specific earthly example of God's *eternal* covenant with us. God does not quit. Did He give up on the children of Israel as they wandered through the wilderness? Has He given up on the church? God does not quit. He does not want an imperfect married couple to quit. That's not part of the script.

We've all heard the complaints.

"I've had it."

"I'm giving up."

"I have nothing more to give to this marriage."

"I'm throwing in the towel."

They're the words of a spouse who has no more hope or energy or desire to give to the marriage. They're ready to surrender, to give in to divorce. The phrase "throw in the towel" is an expression from the early days of boxing. When a fighter was so beaten up and exhausted that he had nothing more to give, a white towel was thrown into the ring to signify he had given up and was willing to concede defeat. But the towel was never thrown in by the fighter himself. It was tossed in by his corner man, his *manager*. *He* made the decision, not the fighter.

When one of us is thinking of throwing in the towel on our marriage, it's really not our decision to make. In fact, too often this decision is made without consulting the Manager of our life. Perhaps we do this because we know what our Manager would say.

We need to see marriage the way Dr. William Doherty does:

Marriage with the long view comes with the conviction that nothing will break us up, that we will fight through whatever obstacles get in our way, that if the boat gets swamped we will bail it out, that we will recalibrate our individual goals if they get out of alignment, that we will share leadership for maintaining and renewing our marriage, that we will renovate our marriage if the current version gets stale, that if we fight too much or too poorly we will learn to fight better, that if sex is no longer good we will find a way to make it good again, that we will accept each other's weaknesses that can't be fixed, and that we will take care of each other in our old age. This kind of commitment is not made just once, but over and over through the course of a lifetime. We cling to it during the dark nights of the soul that come to nearly every marriage, times when the love is hard to feel but the promise keeps us together.[2]

Marriage vows are a prototype of God's pledge never to leave us. When God created the universe, His creative acts were punctuated by the expression, "He saw that it was good." With one exception. He looked at the first human and said, "It's not good that man be alone." And so male and female were created to be with one another. And this *was* good.

But another expression of marriage has emerged during the last forty to fifty years. It's been called the "divorce boom," and many have said, "This is good." It's even been said that this trend is evidence that couples are placing *greater* importance on marriage rather than less—they just don't want to remain in unsatisfactory marriages but instead hope to create another one that *is* fulfilling. But this belief has proved false since most new marriages have also failed to deliver the desired results.

What we now have is "marriage in retreat," and not just because of divorce. Many have tried the alternative of not marrying. Living together, the great American experiment, has now been in place for years. But it, too, has not delivered on its promise.

Advocates for Marriage

The alternatives have become so common, *The Wall Street Journal* reports that long-term marriage is the new status symbol. Americans continue to say that a happy marriage is the number one goal—in fact, 85 to 90 percent of Americans are still choosing to marry.[3]

And yet we hesitate in our churches to speak of the standard of "one marriage" under God, even in a loving and positive way. Could it be that we fear offending or discomforting those who are divorced or in a second or third marriage? If the church doesn't hold to God's standard and at the same time show how this is possible, who will?

So how do we respond to those we know who share with us they are ending their marriage? Do we say, "You know, if I were in your situation I wouldn't stand for that either"? Or, "You deserve better—you deserve to be happy"?

Do you like rejection? I don't. Few of us cultivate rejection. We want others to like us and accept us. But we can go too far to make that happen, even to the extent of offering advice that runs counter to Scripture. If anything, we're called to live counter to our culture, but the church has moved in the opposite direction. We're quiet when we should speak up. We're willing to remain neutral instead of taking a stand that is unpopular. And as individuals, we are overly focused on our own marriages to the extent that we are willing to let others disintegrate.

When we hear through the grapevine that a friend or church member is going to divorce, we often maintain a posture of uneasy silence. We hope they don't talk to us about it, because that would generate tension. On the one hand we don't want to see the couple split and feel that it's wrong, but on the other hand we don't want to offend anyone. So instead, by our silence, we contribute to our divorce-friendly culture.

Whatever happened to "Let's intervene and *help* them find a better way"?

What if we said to the troubled couple, "I hear your concern, but do you believe you've given this marriage 150 percent?

Have you pulled out all the stops and sought consistent professional counseling?"

What about turning to God's Word and saying, "Let's study what God says about divorce"?

I've seen greatly distressed and troubled couples experience restoration and healing. It's possible. It can and does happen.

Years ago, two books were published—*Know What You Believe* and *Know Why You Believe*—that helped many Christians understand church doctrine and the core beliefs of our faith. These books explained the reasons for believing what we believe. These titles are also relevant for those of us who are married. What do you believe about marriage? Have you ever stopped to consider what you believe about it? Most haven't. They're just married. But *why* are they married? Why is it so important?

We need more couples who know why they're married.

We need more couples who indeed are *advocates* for marriage.

We need couples who are willing to speak out for this God-given institution.

As a society and as a church, we have taken marriage for granted. We've allowed states and the federal government to water it down and give to others recognition and benefits that exclusively belong to those who are married.

We assume our children will marry. But what if they become soured on marriage because of what they've seen in other marriages and in our nation? Perhaps they'll choose to live with someone, stay single, and still have a child. If your children were to come to you and say, "All right, convince me that marriage is the way to go," what would you say? By the time you finish this book you'll be able to answer this question in a new and powerful way.

Marriage Keepers

Promise Keepers, a call to spiritual commitment for men, is one of the most positive movements to sweep across this country in recent decades. Out of this ministry came a smaller movement called Marriage Keepers, which is designed to strengthen marriages. A few years ago I participated with this group in conducting a marriage enrichment seminar on a cruise to Alaska. I was intrigued with this idea of being a Marriage Keeper and its implications for our own marriages, as well as others. (Another writer has discussed this concept, although more from what the church can do rather than individuals. See chapter 9 of *Getting Marriage Right* by David Gushee, Baker Books.)

What does marriage keeping mean, and how does it translate into practice? We need to first look at the word *keeping*. We find it used in the early chapters of Genesis 4, where Abel *kept* flocks. It has the broader meaning of looking after something or someone with care and concern. It's also used in Genesis 6, where Noah took animals on the ark and kept them alive. The word as used there means "preserving life." Another use involves keeping covenant obligations before God (see Exodus 20:6; Deuteronomy 8:2)—that is, faithfully obeying, observing, and performing our covenant obligations. Several passages in the New Testament carry the same idea of obeying the law and its obligations (see, for example, John 8:51; Ephesians 4:3;

James 1:26; and Peter 3:16). The meaning here involves preserving, guarding, holding on to, obeying, and fulfilling.

Marriage keeping involves preserving, caring for, and honoring marriage.[4] This is a commitment to do whatever it takes, not just for our own marriage, but for others, too. It means being available to help when other couples need you or, to be blunt, intervening in a troubled relationship *even when uninvited*. It means honesty in modeling our own marriages so couples feel free to say to us, "We need help." In a series on marriage at my own church, our pastor shared very openly, saying, "As many of you know, my wife and I have had difficulty in our marriage, mainly because we were both difficult people." He went on to describe some of the adjustments they had made to get where they are now.

Being a Marriage Keeper means being on a mission—to demonstrate that God's plan for marriage works, to call others to experience it according to His plan, and to rescue those on the brink of disintegration. Few have ever considered that marriage is a missionary enterprise of the church. I've heard some say, "Let others handle their marriage. I have my own to keep intact. I'm not going to meddle."

But we don't have a choice. We have a mandate to model a marriage in progress, imperfect but growing because Christ is made central in the relationship. And if we say that Jesus Christ makes a difference in our marriage, people will watch us, just as they will keep an eye on anyone who chooses to live a lifestyle counter to their culture. As G. K. Chesterton said, "[Marriage] is the theater of the spiritual drama."[5]

This is all right. Expect it. Jesus said, "Let your light shine before men, that they may see your good deeds and praise your Father in heaven" (Matthew 5:16). The authors of *Marriage Made in Eden* have written:

> We are called to be God's people *in* the world, an unavoidable alternative, a visible presence, a persuasive voice. We are mandated to do good deeds with the goal that people may see and give glory to God who is in heaven.
>
> Two women out shopping paused to look at an elegant pair of shoes displayed in the window of an upscale shoe store. One woman commented to her companion, "Just look at those shoes! It takes an Italian to make a shoe like that." As God's people, we are called to live within the culture in such a way that the watching world may see our lives and say, "Now it takes a Christian to make a marriage like that."[6]

Not only do we all need to reach out to others, we need to allow others to reach out to us when we struggle. Some couples are wonderful givers but resistant receivers. It could be pride or fear that blocks us, but when your marriage is in need, be receptive.

As a counselor, I'm involved with crisis intervention teams. In times of tragedy or trauma we go in to help the victims and offer assistance for recovery. We do this after the fact. But when it comes to marriages, the church needs crisis intervention teams to somehow intervene *before* a marriage breaks apart.

I know a number of couples who almost divorced but

recovered, including couples nearly torn apart by adultery but who experienced God's forgiveness as well as one another's. These restored couples often have developed highly refined intuitive antennae and can pick up signs of possible problems in other couples. They come alongside a troubled pair, develop a relationship, and are able to intervene before disaster strikes. These courageous couples openly share in churches, conferences, and classes the path they took and the steps that led to the near disaster in their own marriage. They are willing to say to others, "Some of you are walking that same path, and some of you are already there. We'd like to talk with you because if we were able to turn it around, you'll be able to as well. It's not too late." And couples come to them. Why? Because they understand. They've been there. They offer hope because they're Marriage Keepers.

My hope is that this book will lead you to become a Marriage Keeper for the sake of your own marriage and for others. I hope to share with you a greater understanding and appreciation of God's plan for marriage, and that you will be able to articulate to others the pitfalls of society's alternatives.

Does this sound overwhelming? Perhaps.

But attainable? Definitely.

Chapter Two

THE SCRIPT

IN THE FILM INDUSTRY every studio is hopeful that each film they produce will become a box office sensation. When a film they release is seen by millions, the studio makes millions. A major hit is often referred to as a "blockbuster." In fact, one of the largest video rental chains is called Blockbuster and their stores carry all the big hits.

Films touch us, influence us, tap into our emotions and beliefs, and offer relief from the drudgeries of the real world. Movies start trends in clothing styles, recreational activities, music, even in what we drive. They show us what it's like to live with hope or without hope. Sometimes the realities of life are portrayed very realistically; other times, movies offer pure escapism. I know. I was raised on them.

For me and my family, growing up in Hollywood during

the forties and fifties, going to the movies was a once- or twice-weekly event. Like most of America, we went to the movies to be entertained. And like everyone else, we had our favorite actors and actresses. We rarely paid attention to the other names on the credits, and I don't recall ever choosing a film based on the director or producer or writer. But we did like big movies from the big studios—MGM, RKO, Paramount—that told big stories and promised big entertainment. We wanted to see blockbusters.

Recently, our pastor began a series on marriage titled *Blockbuster Marriages: Writer, Director, and Producer—God.* This is what we all want—a blockbuster marriage, an exceptional marriage. And it's possible to have one because, as the cast, we've been given the most important ingredient: We have the script from the Writer, Director, and Producer. But like haughty, undisciplined actors and actresses on a film set, we sometimes change the scenes and the lines without informing anyone else. This kind of behavior throws everyone off balance, delays production, raises the cost of the film, and generates tension among the other participants.

The reason most couples struggle in their marriage is because somewhere, somehow, they've changed the script and fired or ignored the Director. They have their own ideas about what a marriage should do and how it should work, and so they're content to follow their amateurish ideas and reject a storyline that works. God has a plan for every marriage—a plan to fulfill a grand purpose—and marriage works best when you commit to following the script and the Director. That's what we're going to look at together—the script.

Scenes from a Marriage

One common problem is that so many of us are concerned first with our own personal happiness and self-fulfillment in marriage and *then* with the happiness of our spouses. We want our partner to please *us*. I've heard some say, "No, that won't work. Reverse it. Turn it around. Your first priority is the happiness of your partner. You're to please *him* [or her]."

Wrong on both counts. The apostle Paul said it should be our goal to please God (see 2 Corinthians 5:9). I know, it's a different way to look at our marriage, but daily we need to consider what we do and say and ask, *Is this something that will be pleasing to Jesus Christ?* Puts a different slant on the relationship, doesn't it?

Instead, most of us in marriage are asking, *Will this satisfy me? How can I be fulfilled? What will please me and make me happy? And, oh yes, what would please my spouse?*

I wonder what the state of our unions would be if we started each day by asking, *What would please God today in my marriage? What words, what thoughts would please Him?* What if we asked these questions again before seeing our spouse at the end of the day? Questions such as these take our focus away from ourselves and help us to focus instead on Jesus. If we are to live out the New Testament, we need to be following the words of Paul: "Those who live should no longer live for themselves but for him who died for them and was raised again" (2 Corinthians 5:15). I suggest you write these questions on a card and place it on your bedside table. Memorize this Scripture. Pray that God would give you what you need to live out His script.[1]

When we marry for personal happiness and satisfaction, and then, for whatever reason, these begin to diminish or never met our standards to begin with, we tend to begin entertaining all sorts of unconstructive thoughts. I've heard people complain, "Why didn't He make men and women different than He did? It would make marriage so much easier." But why should God make it easier? Did He create marriage to make us happy or to make us holy?[2]

I talked with a couple in their late twenties who had been married for five years. In the third year they had considered divorce. This is what they told me:

> We entered marriage with high hopes and great expectations. Finally, we'd found someone that would make us happy. I had this dream but it ended up being more like a vapor. She didn't measure up, and neither did I. We always wanted more. We wanted the other to be better. We began to criticize and demand: "You're not meeting my needs. You're not the person I thought I was marrying." And then one of us mentioned the *D* word. We looked at one another and said, "No, never. There's got to be a better way."
>
> So we began to ask, *What does God want for our marriage?* After a hard two years, we've discovered a new way of living. Each morning we ask, "What *will* please God in our marriage today?" The more we do this, the more satisfied we are with one another. The other way didn't work. This does. I'm just sorry we didn't start out that way.

The purpose of marriage is to please God. We need to remind ourselves of this each day, then take note of our words and actions and ask, *Does this please Him?* This is a safeguard. It provides a hedge of protection around a marriage.

Strong Christian marriages will still be struck by lightning—sexual temptation, communication problems, frustrations, unrealized expectations—but if the marriages are heavily watered with an unwavering commitment to please God above everything else, the conditions won't be ripe for a devastating fire to follow the lightning strike.

If I'm married only for happiness, and my happiness wanes for whatever reason, one little spark will burn the entire forest of my relationship. But if my aim is to proclaim and model God's ministry of reconciliation, my endurance will be fireproof.[3]

Your Spouse Is Made in His Image

Let's look further at the script. In the beginning there was nothing. No moon, no sun, no earth, no man or woman. But then God began to create, and create He did:

Then God said, "Let us make man in our *image*, in our likeness, and let them rule over the fish of the sea and the birds of the air, over the livestock, over all the earth, and over all the creatures that move along the ground." So God created man in his own *image*, in the *image* of God he created him; male and female he created them. (Genesis 1:26–27, emphasis mine)

God commanded and we were created. We're not just the result of His creation but the *delight* of His glory. God said, "It is good." He delighted in His creation as we are to delight in our spouse. Creation is a reflection of the character of God, and creation reflects God's glory. Genesis 1 teaches that you and your spouse are the high point of glory in creation. Remember *that* the next time you speak to your spouse.

Both men and women are made in the image of God, but what does that mean? In biblical times the kings of the East ruled large areas, but travel then was limited. They knew they couldn't be everywhere, so in place of their physical presence they erected statues of themselves in all the major cities. When the residents looked at the statues they were reminded of the one who ruled over them. The statue wasn't the same as the king but was due the same honor and glory. If you dishonored or defaced the statue, it was the same as doing it to the king himself—an act of treason.

You and I are to treat each other with this same respect. You and your spouse are dim reflections of God. You reflect the glory of God.

When I consider your heavens, the work of your fingers, the moon and the stars, which you have set in place, what is man that you are mindful of him, the son of man that you care for him? You made him a little lower than the heavenly beings and crowned him with glory and honor. You made him ruler over the works of your hands; you put everything under his feet: all flocks and herds, and the beasts of the field, the birds of the air, and the fish of the sea, all that swim the paths of the seas. O LORD, our Lord, how majestic is your name in all the earth! (Psalm 8:3–9)

Dr. Martin Luther King Jr. said, "I have a dream." So does God—for your marriage. And you need to discover this and experience the same. We all need to discover God's design for marriage, not our own. You see, marriage matters to God. He had a purpose in mind when He created marriage. God had two relational goals in mind. First, He created a person in His image so that He and the image-bearer could be in fellowship together. Then, seeing the aloneness of this first image-bearer, God made another like the first *and* like God so they could *both* be in fellowship with each other *and* with Him.

God has a plan—and it happens in marriage—for transforming each of us into *image-bearers*. We are called to reflect the glory of God in the marriage relationship. Unfortunately, this is not what most couples have in mind as their purpose when they enter into marriage.

Remember, God's main purpose is not our happiness. Happiness is a by-product that occurs when you follow the main theme. We need to follow the script. My pastor, Dave Champness, put it this way: "God has a plan for your marriage that will bring deep love, happiness, intimacy; but if you make your happiness your primary priority, you will miss it all. His plan is to use your marriage to reflect His glory and make you whole, and *then comes happiness*. If we look to our marriages to fulfill our own ideas or expectations, we often meet with disappointment or disillusionment."

Our task is to commit to following the script.

Your marriage is not only going to change you; it will transform you. Consider the term "whistle-blower." Depending on who's doing the talking, the phrase may be said with appreciation or scorn. It's a term used to describe someone who has revealed or exposed the truth about a person or a situation. A whistle-blower brings to light what was previously hidden. That's what marriage is, a whistle-blower. Marriage exposes and reveals who you really are when you enter into that covenant relationship. All the hidden places—and yes, defects too—will be made obvious. You'll be "found out." But that's all right. What a wonderful place for the process of transformation to occur!

Transformation—it's an interesting word. Transformation is at the heart of marriage. Yet many Christian couples have never integrated a pattern of Christian growth into their marriage. This is unfortunate since the two are so closely intertwined. They really can't run alongside one another on parallel tracks.

Scripture says we are to be conformed to the image of Christ (see Romans 8:29) and that Christ is to be formed in us (see Galatians 4:19). The results of this process should be evident in the marriage relationship. They're part of the script.

Both of you, you and your spouse, are quite different but equal in the eyes of God. In the New Testament, Paul reiterates this when he says that in Christ there is neither male nor female (see Galatians 3:28). This impacts the way you are to treat one another. We're called to glorify one another, not degrade.

Our only option in all encounters is to glorify or degrade. We degrade when we violate the other person's glory or when we use the other's glory for our own purpose. Violation of glory involves any form of emotional, physical, or sexual harm. When a husband verbally demeans his wife or when a wife withdraws from involvement with her spouse, they violate each other, degrade one another.

Men and women must trust each other as who we are: God's representatives on earth. If we degrade, abuse, or neglect one another, we insult the very glory of God. Like the psalmist, we should be on the edge of wonder as we consider other people.[4]

If we were to see our spouse as someone to be used or abused, we're not responding to our spouse to the glory of God. We can insult the image of God in other, more simple ways as well. A friend of mine described it in very practical terms: "When you take someone for granted, you demean him or her. You send the unspoken message, *You are not worth much to me.* You also rob this person of the gift of human appreciation. And to be loved and appreciated gives all of us a reason to live each day."

When that gift is withdrawn or denied over the years, a person's spirit begins to wither and die. A couple may endure this hardship and stay married for decades, but they are only serving a sentence. In long-term marriages where one spouse or both are continually taken for granted, a wall of indifference arises between husband and wife. The longer the marriage, the higher the wall and the greater the human isolation. The way out of this woodpile is simple but crucial:

- Start saying *thank you* and showing appreciation for anything and everything.
- Become more consciously tuned to what is going on around you.
- Become more giving and affirming toward your spouse.
- Specialize in the many things that mean a lot: Bring each other flowers. Take long walks in the country. Lie on the floor in front of the fireplace. Prepare breakfast in bed for each other. Hold hands in public and walk in the rain. Send caring and funny cards to each other in the mail. Buy each other small gifts for no apparent reason.

Remember, a thirty-five-year marriage does not guarantee a year number thirty-six. Take nothing for granted just because you have it today.[5]

Revealing God's Glory in Your Spouse

Many come to the end of their marital journey with more regrets than positive memories. We're always building one or the other. Sometimes it takes just a few moments to build an encounter that lasts forever.

For a number of years we conducted an autumn marriage enrichment seminar in the Grand Teton National Park in Wyoming. You couldn't ask for a more peaceful and beautiful location. There were very few tourists that time of year, and the fall colors were exploding on the trees. One evening after the meeting at the lodge, my wife and I got into our car for the short drive back to our cabin. On the radio a popular male singer was performing a melodic love song. Snow had just started to fall and you could look up and see the individual flakes. When we arrived at the cabin, I turned off the motor and we sat there in silence listening to the end of the song and looking out at the intensifying snowfall. After a while we left the car and went inside. Later that evening we both remarked, "Wasn't that a special time, just sitting in the car?" To this day, we've remembered that special time of connecting when no words were said or needed.

One of the high points of splendor for most couples is the wedding ceremony. But hand in hand with this day of joy comes society's constant portrayal of marriage as a trap that is boring, painful, and in some cases, a living nightmare. But society does not see the wedding as the onset of marriage as it's meant to be—a bringing together of two image-bearers.

A marriage is the most powerful of all relationships. You and your spouse will either enhance and give the glory to the other or degrade and/or steal the glory of the other. Are you enhancing the glory in your spouse?[6] Can you think of ways of doing this? Most of us have never thought about this. Look at your husband or wife. What do you see? Do you see the glory of God there? Do you see a unique reflection of God? Enjoy the reflection of God's glory in your spouse. Honor it. Enhance it. When you are married you can both enjoy and shape the glory of God in the other as no other person can.[7]

What does this mean? Your marriage relationship comes

with a challenge—to take the raw material you each have to reveal more of the glory of God. That's a far cry from what most of us are focused on.

You're called to create, so create. How? By serving, loving, and living out Scripture in a way that your spouse is built up. You're to glorify God by drawing the best out of your spouse— not the worst but the richer, the treasure. There is untapped, undeveloped potential in your spouse that, with your help, can surface and grow.

Jean told her husband, John, "You have a depth of compassion and empathy within. I see it in your eyes and your posture. That's a gift from God. Right now you're not sure how to express it. If you had the words or could use word pictures, you could do wonders for those around you. I'd like to help if you would allow me to at your pace and your timing." John couldn't refuse an offer like that. Jean was bringing out the glory of God in her husband.

Because every husband and every wife has a sin nature, they will tend to struggle against themselves and against one another. Dan Allender says, "Marriages suffer under the freight of the Fall." There are many challenges, such as work, time, and in-laws, that can eat away at a relationship and cause each to forget he or she is made in the image of God and that their calling is to assist the other in bringing out the glory of God. Allender goes on to say, "We struggle with sin in every dimension of every relationship, but in marriage we struggle with it more intensely and with more potential for damage."[8]

It's true that there was deep trouble in the Garden of Eden. The first relationship was a broken relationship.

Then the man and his wife heard the sound of the LORD God as he was walking in the garden in the cool of the day, and they hid from the LORD God among the trees of the garden. But the LORD God called to the man, "Where are you?"

He answered, "I heard you in the garden, and I was afraid because I was naked; so I hid."

And he said, "Who told you that you were naked? Have you eaten from the tree that I commanded you not to eat from?"

The man said, "The woman you put here with me—she gave me some fruit from the tree, and I ate it."

Then the LORD God said to the woman, "What is this you have done?"

The woman said, "The serpent deceived me, and I ate." (Genesis 3:8–13)

You and I still suffer because of this initial crisis of mankind. But in spite of the struggle we can still reflect God's image today.

My friend Tim asked me one day, "I understand all this stuff about image-bearing and being holy and all that, but how do I know if I'm doing it or even getting close? Do you have an image thermometer?"

A good question.

I don't know how much courage you have, but the suggestion I'm going to make will definitely measure it. The first question won't take much courage to answer, but just wait for the second one. I borrowed it from a speaker who said that if couples honestly considered and answered this question throughout their married lives, they would rarely, if ever, need to go for marriage counseling.

So the first question to ask yourself is, *What is it like being married to me?* Take some time to reflect on this question. Take a day, or better yet, take a week and carry a three-by-five-inch index card around with you. And when a thought comes to mind, write it down. Asking yourself a question like this is like looking into a mirror. You'll see areas where you can say, "I'm doing all right there." But you'll discover others areas where you'll say, "I need some work." [9]

Now the hard question.

Ask your *spouse* to answer this question for you: "What is it like being married to me?" Have him or her take several days to process the question before answering. And if you really want some help, you could ask, "In what area or areas would you like to see some improvement?" If you ask this, assure your spouse that no matter what they suggest all you will say is, "Thank you for letting me know."

I'm going to repeat this question again and again in this book. In fact, you may feel haunted by it. You may feel like hiring a ghostbuster to get rid of it. Let it haunt you day and night. The answers to this question will let you know about your effectiveness as an image-bearer—and help strengthen you in your role as a Marriage Keeper.

Picture This

If we were to draw a picture of a marriage that functions well, with each person feeling fulfilled, what would the spouses be doing or saying? I think we would see a picture of two spouses allowing each other to develop to their full potential, to become all that God intends for each of them to become.

Both would work to reflect what they believe from the Scriptures. But are you aware of what this really involves? Have you asked yourself, *What do I need to do to better reflect the glory of God's image within me, to become all that God wants me to become and to reflect the effect of Scripture on my life within my marriage?*

That's what marriage is about. It's not a time to just kick back and expect to be waited on or catered to. Nor is your marriage just going to "happen." No, you each need to take an attitude of allowing yourselves to be stretched. You're called by God to grow in ways you never dreamed of. It means you make a decision to develop competence in areas in which you were previously uninterested or untalented. It means taking the risk of learning something new and perhaps falling flat on your face at first.

Few of us want to step out into an area of discomfort. But we need to begin to seek out ways to better serve our spouse, to make their life easier and to better meet their needs. Our calling in marriage is not to dump our responsibilities onto our spouse and make their life and workload heavier, but to reach into their life and lighten it. It means a husband no longer waits to be asked by his wife to help around the house or with the children, but instead learns to look and listen for what could be done and does it. A wife may begin to consider what she expects her husband to do that she could learn to do herself and works to develop her ability in this area.[10]

Remember that happiness and fulfillment are merely by-products.

There's one other way we can do this. We can consciously practice "marriage first." For many, this concept is foreign since their marriage is "just there," a part of life that in many ways is left unattended, like a flowerbed gradually being overtaken by weeds.

After a few years some marriages just begin to drift. And when drifting occurs you get into trouble. On one of our early trips to the Grand Teton National Park, eight of us decided to take some rafts and float the Snake River ourselves. We had been on several guided trips before and felt we could handle this section since there were no real rapids or whitewater. We drove to the launching area, blew up the rafts with what we thought was enough air, and to test their buoyancy had one of the couples get into the raft. Well, the man weighed three hundred pounds, and when he and his wife sat down the raft folded up around them like a set of jaws. We should have seen that as an omen for the remainder of the trip.

We pumped up the rafts with more air and set out with four people in each raft. After several miles of slowly drifting, we decided to lash the two rafts together with ropes so we could talk together more easily. Now, rafts have no rudders and paddles are the only way to steer—it's easy just to drift where the currents take you. There didn't seem to be a problem with this. That is, until we spotted another stream pouring into our river, thus increasing its intensity.

By now it was raining and we were getting tired. When our tied-together rafts hit the convergence of these two rivers, we took off like a shot. We were at the mercy of the current and couldn't steer the rafts. Wouldn't you know it, right ahead of us was a logjam. One raft wanted to go to one side of the jam and one to the other side—so we compromised and hit the logjam head-on. We were stuck, so I took out my knife and slashed the ropes, freeing the other raft. It proceeded to float another hundred yards before it sank in three feet of water, and those in the raft walked to shore. But we were really stuck until the other rafters waded out and gave us a hand.

It was a memorable trip, to say the least. Afterward, we all went to dinner at the lodge and reminisced for two hours while watching lightning bounce off the peaks of the mountains. We all came to the same conclusion: We got into difficulty because we were just drifting without rudders to guide us; we had given no thought to the obstacles or problems that might occur later on in our journey.

It's very much like many marriages I've seen—drifting every which way, with no planning or purpose.

A lasting marriage requires continual conscious effort, and you may have to retrain your mind or write this on a card and review it with your morning devotions. Each day tell yourself anew (I know of couples who say this to one another), "Today I'm going to say 'I do' all over again by considering our marriage in every choice I make."

Can you do this? Will you do this?

This is a reminder of your marriage commitment. You need to remember that fulfilling God's calling to serve Him and reflect His image is dependent upon fulfilling your commitment and protecting the privacy of your marriage. You're helping your spouse, and your spouse is helping you, to become the person God wants each of you to become. Each day you have a fresh opportunity to let your spouse know how important his or her presence is in your life.[11]

Live by the script and remember who *is* the Writer, the Producer, and the Director.

For Your Consideration

1. Ask yourself each morning, *What is it like being married to me?*
2. Ask this of yourself again before the end of each day.

Chapter Three

"ME" OR "WE"?

THEY BOTH SAT in my office with disgusted expressions. Kurt said, "I guess we must be setting some kind of record— married only four months and here we are seeing a marriage counselor. I can't believe it. Only four months and the honeymoon is over."

"So that's why you're here? The honeymoon you thought might last for a longer period of time came to an abrupt end?"

They both nodded. I continued, "If you're like many couples, you've had a number of disappointments to contend with. Some of your expectations, dreams, hopes, and fantasies have hit a wall of reality. Right?" Their expressions told me that's exactly what had happened. (Unfortunately, they had married without the extensive premarital counseling program that couples need, which can help avoid many of these difficulties.)

"So right now," I said, "you could be on the brink of a new stage called *devaluation of one another*. One of the reasons it happens is, the more you have exaggerated one another's positive qualities and attributes, when the inevitable defects and disappointments occur, the bigger they are in light of what you had hoped for. Has that been happening?"

Nods from both.

"Now speaking of your honeymoon, it's good that it ended."

Silence.

I went on. "Yes, it's good, because you don't need it anymore. The idealism was there for a while to get you started. A honeymoon is a transition time. It's like a bicycle with a set of training wheels. It gives you extra support in order to get started, but in time you gain skill and confidence and you're ready for a change. The transition may be bumpy, but you soon realize you can do it. The honeymoon love will then grow into a mature, deeper love. And over the years you'll experience other honeymoons far more exciting than what you've just experienced. Your spouse is not any less; they're just less of a stranger than they were."[1]

There's a transition when you marry. Once a couple says "I do," predictability sets in and the adventure of mutual discovery stops. There's no mystery, no more novelty. Conversation that at one time had heart now begins to seem more efficient, more task-oriented, and sometimes just plain automatic.

There's an emotional momentum present during courtship. This is necessary, but it isn't meant to be permanent. The higher the level of expectations, the less a couple really knows one another. The more the idealization of one's partner, the greater the letdown in the first year of marriage. We call this the *stage of disenchantment.* It's normal.

> Disenchantment is healthy, for courtship is the condition of simulated perfection, a game well played by participants who can still choose the times and conditions favorable to its success.[2]

Now real life begins.

The first few years of marriage have been given numerous labels. They have many names, including the "age of discovery." When we talk about someone experiencing a crisis, it's called the "impact stage." It refers to a time of being overwhelmed or thrown off balance or being thrown into a state of confusion. Some refer to it as a time of disillusionment. Whatever the label, it's a time of opening our eyes to reality rather than fantasy. It's the first year of marriage!

What was it like for you? That first year was a stage-setter. Patterns and interactions were established during this time of discovery that set the tone for your relationship in the ensuing years. What discoveries do you remember from that first year?

Listen to a couple named Adelle and Tim:

> We talked about our first year before we ever married and agreed on several items. We agreed that we not only didn't know one another as well as we thought, but we also didn't know ourselves as well as we thought. So we told each other, "You're going to help me know myself better, and I will be doing the same for you."

We also asked one another, "What are ten small habits you have which are likely to surprise or amaze me?" Most of what we shared at this time came true, but it wasn't such a hassle. The surprise element was gone and often our reaction was, "So that's what you meant. I can handle that."

We also learned to ask ourselves the question, *How important is this issue, really?* In light of what matters, especially the spiritual, it put things in perspective. I wanted us to accept each other as we really are—imperfect and flawed. God sees us as valuable in this state, so why should we try to improve on His perspective?

Every couple discovers a few surprises during their first year. But to hear them talk or read books about this, the focus always seems to be negative. Without living in denial it's time to put a gag rule on the negative and talk about the pleasant discoveries instead. Why not reflect back on your first year? What were some of the delightful discoveries you made? What were the pleasant surprises? What about in the last five years? The positives are too often overlooked, ignored, or neglected, which in time deadens your thoughts and feelings for your spouse.

Celebrating Your Differences

If we don't concentrate on what is working in our relationship, what is going well, what is good, we'll soon drift into a mindset that results in asking the question, *Did I really marry the right person?* Has that thought ever flown into your mind? Possibly.

But think about this.

You married the right person.

It's true. If you're married, you *did* marry the right one. No other person will be the "right" person. Even when you're upset with one another, angry, disillusioned, or needs aren't met, you've married the right one. A new relationship won't be the answer, no matter how much you tell yourself it will. Why? Because it's doubtful that anyone can fulfill all your needs the way you want. There is only One who can and will satisfy, and that is the Lord.

Somebody once said that whether you married the right person or the wrong person is up to you. You may have married the right person, but if you treat them like the wrong person, that's what they become. But if you marry the wrong person and treat them like the "right" person, that's who you end up with. So whether you married the "right" or "wrong" person is up to you.

When the "wrong person" mentality gains a foothold, you begin to think, *We have irreconcilable differences, so we had better call it quits*. This excuse is given time and time again at divorce proceedings. Irreconcilable differences are *not* a reason for this unbiblical action. We all live with some "irreconcilable differences," since no man and woman are exactly alike. Clones we're not, and we wouldn't care for it if we were. Differences are not the problem. It's how you interpret them, how you label them, whether you see them as friend or foe, whether they're seen as something that will drain you or replenish you.

Dr. Phil, the talk-show host who has become a household name, struggled with these differences:

> I am embarrassed to confess to you how many years I spent being frustrated with my wife, judging and resisting her for doing exactly what God designed her to do. God didn't design us to be the same; he designed us to be different. He made us different because we have different jobs in this world, and yet we criticize each other for being who we are.[3]

Your job is to identify these differences and learn to celebrate them. Differences can be an exchange of strengths. Each of you needs one another's differences. See them as an opportunity to be stretched rather than confined. It's true that some of these differences can prove to be irritants and sometimes inconvenient, but that's looking at just one side of them.

You see, no marriage is ever what a person expects it to be. Real life can never compete with the dreams and fantasies conjured by the mind. In marriage you gain as well as lose, but both experiences can be positive. In a divorce-friendly culture it's all too easy to exchange the old for something new. But the new relationship will come with its own set of gains and losses—usually more losses. Marriage is two unfinished people coming together and each helping to complete and refine the other. That's what Marriage Keeping is all about.

Our "me" culture leads many couples to face the challenges of marriage from a position of narcissism. Many couples never make the "we" connection that is the heart of marriage, and they continue to perform the "me" dance, which is contrary to God's plan for us. Marriage is simply a call to servanthood, not personal fulfillment or happiness. Each day we need to be reminded of the scriptural mandate, "Do not look out only for yourselves. Look out for the good of others also" (1 Corinthians 10:24, NCV).

God's Word, His script, is the foundation for the early years of marriage, as well as each succeeding year.

> Don't become so well-adjusted to your culture that you fit into it without even thinking. Instead, fix your attention on God. You'll be changed from the inside out. Readily recognize what he wants from you, and quickly respond to it. Unlike the culture around you, always dragging you down to its level of immaturity, God brings the best out of you, develops well-formed maturity in you. (Romans 12:2, *The Message*)

One of the ways you, as a couple, must act that runs counter to our cultural tendency is to develop a "we" rather than "me" mentality. God's plan is to bring the two of you together and for you to stand as a unit. But that's not what our culture is saying. Advertisers and media daily reinforce the message, "Look out for yourself. Be sure to meet your own needs." How do you take that attitude into marriage and survive? You don't. This attitude has to change, but with little track record of living this way, it's a major adjustment.

But God says it is possible. He wouldn't have created marriage if it weren't. (Can you identify when "me" still creeps into your marriage?) In marriage your lives are commingled. You don't lose your identity, but self-centered isolation never works.

Remember one of the first words you learned as a child? (Other than *no*?) *Mine*. That's *mine*. That's not yours, it's *mine*. A preschool child says this a dozen times a day. As adults it's not always so blatant, but the sentiment is there just the same. And if we marry in our twenties or thirties, having always lived for ourselves, it's so easy to enter marriage with a "mine" mindset. It's evident in our choice of car, house, church, career, leisure time, furniture, vacations, etc. And often a power struggle emerges: "mine versus ours" or "me versus us." And it doesn't work. It won't work.

Marriage is more than sharing a life together; it's building a life together. What you do now is for both, and what is said now is for both. What your purpose is now is for the kingdom and giving glory to the image of God.

God's Word says:

> Two are better than one, because they have a good return for their work: If one falls down, his friend can help him up.... Also, if two lie down together, they will keep warm. But how can one keep warm alone? Though one may be overpowered, two can defend themselves. A cord of three strands is not quickly broken. (Ecclesiastes 4:9–12)

I've seen the "me" mindset played out in marriages of twenty, thirty, and even forty years. A cast member who's thinking "me" is not acting according to the script that God has for marriage. When you marry, your perspective and attitude have so much to do with what occurs in your marriage. Sometimes I've heard couples bemoan the fact that they had to give up so much when they married, as though they were stuck looking backward rather than forward. Over the years I've shared with couples in premarital counseling the fact that you can't bring your single lifestyle intact into your marriage. And I ask them, "What will you be giving up?" I ask this to encourage couples to realize that marriage is not something you add on to all of your single activities. Rather, the marriage must become central and other activities take second place.

Here's a healthier attitude as expressed by one wife in her early thirties: "For me, what was left behind needed to be left behind for my growth. I was ready for the changes marriage has made. There are so many gains which have enhanced our life. And because we're married, we're able to experience and do more than if we had remained single. It was a good decision."

Dale's Story

I'd like to tell you about a friend of mine, Dale. We've been friends for more than thirty years. When he was in his early- to midforties, Dale began looking for the right woman to marry. He was thoughtful, selective, and had a definite list of criteria that included a strong walk with the Lord. After several years, some of us began wondering if the woman he was looking for *didn't* exist.

But then it happened. At the age of fifty-two, Dale met Sherry, who was thirty-nine. Dale had said he didn't want to marry anyone who had children, but God had other plans. Sherry had three—ages twenty-one, eighteen, and nine. Years later, Dale said he never realized what a great experience he would have being a stepfather. But I'll let Dale tell you his story:

My wife and I met through the Internet, but really it was through a lot of prayer. God just used that to allow us to find each other. We both had been looking a long time for the right person but never seemed to find the "right one." That was, until I got an e-mail from a nurse in San Diego asking to write her because she thought we might have a number of things in common. I did, and I could tell from her correspondence that her heart was very sincere and that I had found a very special lady.

After writing and talking on the phone for what seemed like weeks, we met in Julian, where she was on a church retreat for the weekend. She proceeded to tell me, as we walked and talked, that at the retreat, while praying, Jesus told her that I was going to marry her. I looked at her, a little surprised, and told her that He hadn't told me. And she said, "Have you asked Him?"

We had such a great first date that we decided to get together again the next day and go for a walk on the beach. She took me to her favorite beach, Del Mar. After walking for a while, she wanted to show me around other parts of Del Mar, so we continued to walk. We went past beautiful parks, art galleries, food places. Then we came to this beautiful church and walked around, looking at the stained glass, where she told me, "I would love to get married someday in this church." Not realizing that this was the church that she already attended and had so many friends at, I told her, "That's nice." Well, six months later we were married in that church— and yes, Jesus did tell me that she was the one.

So after being single for several years following a marriage that didn't last because of deception on the part of his first wife, Dale remarried and moved into the arena of "we" rather than "me." He shared one of his adjustment experiences:

> I was so used to being single, and even being a "married single" in my first marriage, that I didn't give much regard to someone else when I made decisions. I was on my own. But soon after Sherry and I married, I "just" invited my parents and my brother and his wife over for dinner. I told Sherry they were coming over Friday night, and after a few seconds she said, "Dale, I love your family and certainly want them over, but that won't cut it. We need to talk it over with one another first before we make a decision. I won't refuse you. I just want to be included." I needed to learn that it was now "we" and not "me." My old habits needed to change. And I'm glad I had a wife who would help me make this change. "We" is so much better than "me"!

This was one of many learning experiences that Dale and Sherry navigated well. As I watched them and talked with them, it seemed as though they were on a perpetual honeymoon. They grew together, studied together, worked out together, fished and hunted together. The honeymoon went on for three and a half years.

But then Sherry contracted lung cancer and began to go downhill over a period of several months. When the tragic events of 9/11 occurred, I was asked to travel to New York to help debrief survivors. But at God's direction, I remained in California to minister to Dale during the last days of Sherry's life. (I would later minister in New York on five separate occasions.)

Just before Sherry died, she wanted to see her black lab, Molly, one more time. So we marched Molly down the hall into the ICU and put her up on the bed. That was a feat in itself, since Molly was ready to deliver eight pups at any moment. The day before Sherry died, she asked all of her friends to come by. And what she said to everyone was, "The best thing you can do for me is to invite Jesus into your life so we can be together in heaven." The next day she died. Dale asked me to read his eulogy at Sherry's memorial service. Here is a portion of what he had written:

From the time Sherry and I first knew that she had cancer, she knew she was in a battle for her life, but she also felt that she was in a win-win situation. If she lived, she would be able to continue to have a wonderful life here on earth; and if she didn't, she would be in heaven with her Lord. But she really wanted to live with her family. She loved being married, loved me so deeply, and wanted to beat this terrible disease so badly that she underwent chemotherapy, did all kinds of holistic medicines, acupuncture, and even had a special machine she would use for one hour every night that had good results on other types of cancer. She spent a long time daily with God, asking Him to heal her if it was His will. But God had other plans for her.

What Sherry and I had in three and a half years together was packed with so many memories. We thought we were making up for things we missed out on in the past, but we didn't realize we were doing things for the future we wouldn't have together. We had a wonderful time and life together. Neither of us would have changed it for anything, and I would do it over again in a second if God gave me that chance. If there is one thing from this that could be passed on to any couple, it would be to enjoy every minute you have together…as it could be your last.

The psalmist said, "Teach us to number our days aright, that we may gain a heart of wisdom" (Psalm 90:12). Your days together are not limitless. If you can number your days and accept that they are limited, then perhaps you will learn to protect your time together as a couple. One day there will be just one of you left. And you will yearn for more time, but it's gone.

Please don't forget Dale's message. I won't. I pray that his experience will impact your life. It certainly has mine, as I'll share later in this book. Dale and Sherry made their marriage live.

How can you keep your marriage alive?

First, pray. Pray about your relationship and for your spouse. And make time to pray together.

Prioritize your marriage relationship and keep it at the top of your list. Culture won't. Your friends won't. You have to. If you want quality time, you must make it happen. If your marriage is valued, it's because you value it and protect it. It's your choice. A friend of mine said this about a fulfilled marriage:

Happy and fulfilling marriages are products of extreme effort. They are desired, sought after, fought for and planned. They never *just* happen. Couples frequently complain to me how their marriage *just* fell apart. All of a sudden, they just fell out of love. If experience has taught me anything, it is this: Nothing *just* happens, whether good or bad.

Healthy marriages follow a road—a road that is planned. You do not have to plan to fail. That can be accomplished without planning...and usually is. But you DO have to plan to succeed.[4]

Most couples have dreams for their marriage. That's good. Dreams pull us, prompt us, drive us, and give us hope.

June told me about the dream she had for her marriage. The wedding took place in 2001. Two years later she was ready to quit. It "just wasn't working out," she said. And it's not that the dream had turned into a nightmare, as it has for so many; it had just fizzled. We talked.

"Dreams are good," I told her. "We need to dream and dream big if it's realistic. But were you expecting your dream to come true right away? And was it dependent upon what Jim would do or not do?"

There was silence on June's part. She hesitated and said, "Well, yes to both."

"So what was your part in this dream fulfillment, June? What were you doing to make your dream come alive?"

Silence. She left.

I saw June a few weeks later. She said, "I like my dream. It's realistic and it's starting to happen. I've given the dream to God and I'm learning what I need to do. I'm believing in Jim, who he is now, and his potential. I've become his ally and it's working."

I've heard too many over the years say, "Give up your dreams for marriage; if you don't, you'll only be disappointed. Accept what happens and what you get." How pessimistic! How fatalistic!

Are you aware that there's a certain personality type called "the dreamer"? These are highly imaginative people. When they're children they usually frustrate their parents. They color outside the lines and think outside the box. But they often create what hasn't been done before. You don't ever say to a dreamer child, "It can't be done," because they eventually seem to find a way to do *anything* if they try long enough or think hard enough. I wish there were some of the dreamer in every married couple, so they would see their marriage as it *could* be. To see only what *is*—and to therefore settle for marital mediocrity or else give up entirely—is contrary to what God wants for marriage. His calling is not just for couples to stay married but to develop a relationship that reflects His ongoing presence and is mutually fulfilling.

So dream. Dream on! Dream realistically, and dream big for your marriage. Edgar Allan Poe in "Eleonora" wrote, "Those who dream by day are cognizant of many things which escape those who dream only by night."

There's a story of a man whose life was drastically changed when he invited Jesus into his life. Desperate to share his newfound faith, he became a street evangelist and stood on a street corner, proclaiming the truth of Christ. Another man, who was very irritated by what he heard, walked by and said loudly, "Hey! Why don't you shut up? You're just a dreamer."

The street evangelist's twelve-year-old daughter was there and she blocked the way of the irritated man. She said to him, "Mister, I don't know who you are or what your problem is, but that's my father who's preaching. He used to be addicted to alcohol. He'd come home and take my clothes and belongings and sell them to get money for his alcohol. But when God saved him, he got a job, started working, and began buying me clothes and shoes and schoolbooks. He's never drunk another drop of alcohol. Now in his spare time he tells others what God's done in his life. So mister, if my father is dreaming, don't wake him up. Please, please, don't wake him up."[5]

For Your Consideration

1. In what way were you personally unfinished when you married? In what way does your spouse complete you? In what way is your spouse refining you?
2. What behavior did your spouse exhibit during courtship that you would like to see occurring now?
3. Ask yourself, *What is it like being married to me?*

Chapter Four

THE STORY UNFOLDS

LOOK AT THE SCRIPT: "Husbands, love your wives, just as Christ loved the church and gave himself up for her" (Ephesians 5:25). This message has been around for thousands of years, so it's nothing new. But this passage, recited in most traditional wedding ceremonies, is lightly acknowledged by the participants, who have little understanding of its meaning or its application in their own marriages.

The same Scripture passage says a couple of verses earlier, "The husband is the head of the wife as Christ is the head of the church" (v. 23). Sadly, however, too many of us deviate from the Writer's script, instead allowing our culture's ideas of what husbands and wives are to be to dictate our understanding of marriage. The result? Far too many marriages get off track.

To understand and follow the script, we have to shut our ears, eyes, and minds to our culture and focus on God's Word, something too few people are willing to do these days.

Let's face it: If you're following Scripture, you're going the opposite direction on a one-way street with everyone else honking their horns at you and questioning your sanity. But God's Word tells us, "Don't become so well adjusted to your culture that you fit into it without even thinking. Instead, fix your attention on God. You'll be changed from the inside out" (Romans 12:2, *The Message*).

Now, let's take a look at what the script says about what God calls husbands and wives to do and to be.

Called to Lead

According to the script, a husband has three callings, the first of which is to be a leader, or "the head of the wife." But what does that mean? It doesn't mean control, passive noninvolvement, asserted superiority, or taking advantage. On the contrary, a husband must never use his role as leader for selfish benefit. To do so would deviate from the Writer and Director's script.

A husband must never put his wife into a straitjacket of compliance, or she will wither and her love for him will deaden. Even recent secular research has shown that what kills the love of a spouse for the other is in direct violation of Scripture—i.e., attempting to control your partner rather than serve them.

The issue of the man's leadership in the home has been a concern for years. Book after book has been written on this subject, including *Passive Men, Wild Women* and *Husbands Who Won't Lead and Wives Who Won't Follow.* We're talking about biblical headship—specifically the authority of the man to lead.

But there are strings attached.

Ephesians 5:22–23 states, "Wives, submit to your husbands as to the Lord. For the husband is the head of the wife as Christ is the head of the church, his body, of which he is the Savior." This passage endows the authority of a husband's headship, but it also defines and limits it. The analogy of Christ's relationship to the church as the basis for the husband's headship means that the only time he has the right to exercise family authority is when he does it in ways that are consistent with Christ's nature and purpose. Bryan Chapell stated this well when he said, "Headship that transgresses the purposes of God loses God's endorsement."[1]

A man's motives for leading a marriage spiritually can sometimes be mixed, but when he allows God to lead him and when his heart is open to God and His purposes, then his headship receives His support.

So what does that kind of leadership look like in practical terms?

The authority God gives men to lead is built on service. This is a difficult balancing and juggling act for many. The problem is not with the teaching, but with the man who misuses the teaching that he is to lead to serve his own needs and desires. Some men behave like drill sergeants, snapping out orders at their wives and children, which doesn't reflect Scripture but their own selfishness and insecurity.

The truth is, a husband is called to think of others—particularly his wife—first, ahead of himself. That's not easy for many men. For one thing, the idea of being a servant leader runs counter to the thinking in our present-day "me" culture. But with some hard work and sacrifice, it can be done.

I've seen both kinds of leadership. I've seen the self-appointed "dictators" who distort scriptural teaching for their own benefit. The result of this kind of leadership is that marriages and families suffer and fragment. But I've also observed men who are servant leaders, whose families flourished as a result.

Called to Sacrificial Love

God's script also calls the husband to be not just a servant leader but also a lover, meaning that his headship of his family is not to exhibit dominating control but the sacrificial love of Jesus.

And how did Christ love when He was on earth? He was single-minded in His mission of love as He spent time with the disciples and communicated with them, teaching them about forgiveness. He also led by example, helping strengthen the disciples where they were weak. He defended the disciples, praised them before others, and revealed Himself to them. And why did Jesus do these things? Because He was concerned about the church's well-being and future glory.

That is how a husband is to love his wife. A husband represents Jesus in the home, and his role is to bring out God's glory in his wife and lift her up—for *her* well-being. This is leadership that leaves a wife feeling special, valued, and loved.

So how specifically can a husband do that? There are many

ways, one of the most important being a husband's putting his wife first over children, parents, siblings, work, TV, and hobbies. Doing this will strengthen a marriage. But conversely, not doing it will weaken the marriage.

Another thing a loving husband can do is learn his wife's "love language"—in other words, the ways she tends to best express and receive love from others—and package his love in a way that speaks to her and meets her needs.

A husband is also to love his wife unconditionally, the same way God loves all of us. He is not to love her "because she..." but "regardless." When a husband loves his wife sacrificially and unconditionally, then she more fully realizes God's love and regard for her, and this in turn brings glory to Him.[2]

God expects us to care for one another. A husband who neglects or demeans his wife robs her of what God wants for her and robs himself of growth and development as well.

Regarding couples caring for one another, Bryan Chapell wrote:

> Because two people who marry are to be one, if either part damages, demoralizes, or degrades the other, then neither will be completely whole. Just as a basketball deflated on only one side still cannot fulfill its purposes, so a marriage with one side diminished will deprive both persons of fully being and doing what God desires. God has designed the similarities and differences of a man and woman in marriage to complement and support the spiritual growth of both. Neither part to the marriage can develop fully if either one is denied his or

her personal potential.[3]

What an opportunity a husband has! It's very much like Jesus' redemptive work on behalf of the church in that a husband is not to live for himself, but should live to be used as a channel of God's goodness in his wife's life. He is to respond, react, speak, and think toward her in ways that enable her to develop who she is and to develop her gifts as a way to bring glory to God.[4]

An encouraging man does this. He's a man who sincerely tells his wife, "I believe in you," "Go for it," and "How can I help you?"

Called to the Fullness of Christ

We are to do everything in what the Bible calls the "fullness of Jesus Christ," and that includes being married. Colossians 3:15–17 instructs tells us how we can equip ourselves with that fullness:

> Let the peace of Christ rule in your hearts, since as members of one body you were called to peace. And be thankful. Let the word of Christ dwell in you richly as you teach and admonish one another with all wisdom, and as you sing psalms, hymns and spiritual songs with gratitude in your hearts to God. And whatever you do, whether in word or deed, do it all in the name of the Lord Jesus, giving thanks to God the Father through him.

Now let's take a more detailed look at what living in the fullness of Christ means.

Let the peace of Christ rule. This could be paraphrased, "Let the peace of Christ be umpire in your heart amidst the conflicts of life. Let Christ's peace within be your counselor and decide for you what is right." The peace described here is not just the peace you feel when you have no conflict. It is a sense of wholeness and well-being, a sense that God is in control and guiding you.

Who or what rules in your life? The indwelling peace of Christ is indispensable when it comes to blessing your spouse and bringing out God's glory.

Let the word of Christ dwell in you. How do we allow God's Word to take up residence in us? By reading it, studying it, and memorizing it.

I have seen angry people, frustrated people, anxious people, and obnoxious people changed because of the power of God's Word dwelling in them. God's Word has the power to change any of us, and it has power to bring out the best in any marriage.

When you read the Bible, ask the Holy Spirit to make it a part of your life. A chapel speaker I once heard at Westmont College said, "If you take one chapter from the Word of God and read it out loud every day for a month, it will be yours for life." He was right. It works.

Do all in the name of the Lord Jesus. Everything we as Christians do—good or bad—is a reflection of Jesus Christ. Our obedient, loving behavior, including in our marriages, reflects His presence for all the world to see. But when we react and respond in a way contrary to what is in the Scriptures and contrary to our relationship with Jesus, it reflects that He does not fully occupy our lives.

Paul's command to do all in the name of the Lord Jesus follows a series of commands in Colossians 3:5–14. He warns us about behaviors we are to put off because they do not reflect a person who knows Jesus Christ. He tells us to get rid of sexual immorality, impurity, lust, evil desires, greed, anger, rage, malice, slander, filthy language, and lying (vv. 5–9) because none of these behaviors reflects the presence of Christ in our lives. When we engage in any of these things, we've rewritten the script. Ridding ourselves of them will prepare us to do all in the name of Christ.

We are called to replace these negative behaviors with words and deeds that clearly exemplify that we know Christ: compassion, kindness, humility, gentleness, patience, forgiveness (vv. 10–14).

How do you see these positive qualities reflected in your marriage relationship?

Called to Lead—and Love—Sacrificially

A husband is to lead in his marriage by example and sacrificially, not by ordering or constantly instructing his wife. He is never, and I mean *never*, to tell his wife what the Scriptures say *she* is to do. Rather, his only focus is to be on loving his wife as Christ loved the church—that is, sacrificially.

In practical terms, this could mean, among other things, volunteering to bathe the kids or massage his wife's feet, turning off the football game and talking with her, or going shopping with her—even after he's put in a twelve-hour day at work.

Sacrificial love involves participating in something that is important or a favorite of hers, even if it's relatively unimportant to you or definitely not one of your favorites. It may mean doing any of the following (although it's not limited to any or all of them):

- Initiating prayer with her without concern that your prayers may be briefer and more bottom-line than hers.
- Learning to say these three phrases: "You were right," "I was wrong," and "I am sorry."
- Calling her with any delay of plans.
- Practicing Proverbs 31:28–29 (praising her) consistently.
- Accepting her communication style and opinions as different from yours, and not necessarily wrong.
- Accepting her femaleness and celebrating the differences that come from it (see recommended reading).
- Asking for her opinion.
- Discovering the uniqueness of her personality in order to understand her and communicate better (see recommended reading).
- Asking what TV show or movie she would like to watch.

Before we move on: If you're a husband, ask yourself which of these you did this past month. Then ask yourself which of these you will do during the coming month.

Called to Lead by Learning

A few years ago I read an article titled "Study's Advice to Husbands: Accept Your Wife's Influence." The study showed that men who enjoyed the most stable, happy marriages were also likely ones who listened to their wives' suggestions and concerns and followed them. These were men who were willing to learn, change, and grow.[5]

I have found that to be true in my own marriage. Over the years, I have learned that my wife is innately gifted with knowledge, insights, and abilities I don't have. That is probably why the apostle Peter wrote, "[Husbands,] live with your wives in an understanding way…and show them respect" (1 Peter 3:7, NCV), which very simply means that husbands are called on to understand their wives—how they think, how they respond emotionally, and what they need to feel loved and fulfilled in a marriage.

I don't know how many times I've heard men say, "I just don't understand my wife." My response to that is blunt: *You can learn*!

We men can be much worse than lacking in our knowledge of the opposite sex; we can be downright clueless! There is much each and every husband has to learn when it comes to loving their wives. But we can learn, and not only that, we *need* to learn. It's not that difficult, either. It's a matter of taking the time to be a student, a learner, first.

So how can you learn? First, when your wife talks to you, be a listener before you're a fixer. We men tend to want to rush ahead and "fix" situations our wives talk to us about when most of the time, our wives just want us to listen to how they feel about their own situation. For that reason, we should take the time to ask our wives, "Is this a fix-it time or a learning time?"

It goes against the grain of most men to hear this, but I have learned that listening is often one of the best ways to fix things.

Second, be honest with your wife. Don't hide. Share your hurts, your fears, your concerns, your disappointments, your life. Believe me, this will draw the two of you closer than you can imagine. And when you're vulnerable, you're leading in love, and she'll want to follow.

There are many practical things we can do as we seek to learn from our wives. Here are a few of them:

- Invite her into your life and share those things that you think aren't important.
- Ask her about her thoughts, feelings, and opinions.
- At least once a month, take time to reminisce with her about your courtship.
- Call her on your way home to see if she needs anything, such as your child being picked up at school or something from the market.
- Rather than saying "Fine" when your wife asks you how you are doing or how your day was, take the time to really talk to her in depth and with detail.

The Wife's Response

There is today an overabundance of books and ideas inundating our culture about the woman's appropriate role and response to the leadership or headship of her husband. Some, because of their own beliefs or issues with leadership, seem to be trying to reinterpret, rewrite, or delete what the Scripture says on this issue. But that is just as wrong as a man taking what the Bible says about submission and using it as an excuse to act like a drill sergeant.

So what does "Wives, submit to your husbands as to the Lord" mean to you? When you read that, which words do you focus on? In many circles today, the word *submit* is not a popular one. It goes directly against the independence our culture seems to so highly value.

But the key word in this verse isn't *submit*; rather, it's the phrase *as to the Lord.* This means that a woman's motivation to follow is because it's for God's glory that a woman do so—not her husband's.

There are many people now—Christian and non-Christian alike—who can't understand this, nor will they ever consider following it. But the Writer clarifies this teaching in the next verse, "Now as the church submits to Christ, so also wives should submit to their husbands in everything" (Ephesians 5:24).

How does the church fulfill its purposes? By submitting to the will of God. How does a wife fulfill God's purpose for her? By submitting to her husband. This means that submission is an act of worship to God, an act that honors Him. But a wife needs to exercise spiritual discretion and never do anything contrary to the Scripture.[6]

This teaching is found elsewhere—in 1 Peter 3 and in 2 Corinthians 11:7–10, for example. But what exactly does the word *submission* mean? The original word literally meant to "arrange under." Commentators have also interpreted the word in this context to mean "a disposition to yield" or "voluntary yielding in love" or "not to exercise authority over."

Now, what does submission do? The Bible tells us, "For this reason a man will leave his father and mother and be united to his wife, and the two will become one flesh. This is a profound mystery—but I am talking about Christ and the church" (Ephesians 5:31–32). Submission is part of the "oneness" of this verse. It means that in godly, biblical marriage, each spouse gives of themselves for the good of the other.

God has a purpose for your marriage and for you as an individual, but neither will come to pass if you don't care for the fulfillment of one other. Just as a husband helps in the completion of his wife, a wife helps in the completion of her husband. Some men say, "I don't need my wife to complete me." But God says otherwise. He says that you as a husband need your wife as a helper and that He asks her to give you the support and care you need to carry out what you've been called to do. She has gifts that complement you and these help you grow as a godly man.

Submission helps complete the husband. And how? A wife's qualities—her unique gifts and talents—add to the life of the husband. When a wife uses her giftedness, it builds up her husband and brings him glory because it brings out the image of God's glory in him.

In a Christian marriage neither spouse lives or operates for his or her own benefit—it's always for the benefit of one another. It takes work, but it is worth it, for submission is a way we can honor one other. In doing that, however, we need to remember two things: First, we all need to submit ourselves for the good of others God has brought into our lives. Second, this seemingly countercultural response of submission to others doesn't lessen our value or worth.

Respect—What Every Man Needs

Years ago there was a television commercial for a certain brand of car wax. In it a woman was getting ready to sell her car, which looked weathered, old, and dull—so much so that most people wouldn't give it a second look. The woman realized how dull her car looked, so she used this particular brand of car wax on it. Voilà! Her car shone like it was brand-new. It looked so good, in fact, that the woman's affections for it were revived and she decided to keep it.

We and our relationships are a lot like that. When we treat someone as a valued gift and invest ourselves in his or her care, we build up that person's feelings of self-worth *and* draw closer to them as well.[7]

When a wife respects, nurtures, and affirms her husband, it deepens her love for him. On the other hand, when we don't regard something as valuable and neglect it, our feelings for it begin to wane. At the top of any man's list of needs is respect from his mate; God created men that way. He needs respect as much as he needs air to breathe. A man who doesn't receive respect from his wife is a man who begins to wither on the inside. He's all right as long as no one is standing on the air hose running to the tank labeled Respect.[8]

That is exactly why God calls wives to respect their husbands (Ephesians 5:33).

Some believe that respect is something we all must earn. But just like love, respect from spouse to spouse must be unconditional. This is what Scripture teaches: "Show proper respect to everyone...not only to those who are good and considerate, but also to those who are harsh" (1 Peter 2:17–18).

I've seen numerous instances in which a wife began to believe in her husband and showed him respect. The husband, in turn, began to change—both in his own thinking and beliefs and in how he treated and responded to his wife.

How can a wife show respect for her husband? Here are just a few examples:

- Express faith in his decision and ability.
- Leave him notes (men respond better to the written word) that tell him how much you value who he is as a person (and sometimes for his work).
- If he botches a task at home, don't sigh, roll your eyes, and mutter at him; instead, thank him for trying.
- Make positive suggestions without demanding an immediate answer. Ask him to reflect on it for a while.
- Listen to his upsets and don't take his anger personally.
- Let him vent when he needs to.
- Encourage him in areas where he doesn't feel secure and let him know you stand behind him.
- When he makes a decision you're not in favor of, listen.
- Talk about his positive strengths in front of the children.
- Praise him at least once a day.
- Discover the uniqueness of his personality and learn to understand him and communicate better with him.

- Accept his maleness and celebrate the differences that come from this (see recommended reading).

If you're a wife, ask yourself which of these you did this past month in an effort to show your husband respect. Then ask yourself how you'll find ways to do these things in the coming month and beyond.

Here's a good example of a wife showing her husband the respect, admiration, and love he needed from her:

One of the pastors I respected greatly was E. V. Hill, who served for many years as pastor of Mt. Zion Missionary Baptist Church in Los Angeles. When E. V. first began in the ministry, he was a hard worker who wanted to provide for his wife, but he was also a young preacher who struggled to make enough money just to pay for the necessities.

Pastor Hill's wife appreciated his efforts to protect and provide for her, even though some months there wasn't enough money to pay all the bills. One night, he came home and noticed immediately that the house was dark. When he opened the door, he saw that his wife, Jane, had prepared a candlelight dinner. He loved the idea, but when he went to the bathroom to wash up, he flipped the light switch and nothing happened. Then he went to the bedroom and tried the lights. Again...nothing. The entire house was dark.

He went back and asked his wife why the lights didn't work. Jane began to cry and said, "You work so hard, but it's rough. I didn't have enough money to pay the electric bill. I didn't want you to know about it, so I thought we would just eat by candlelight!"

Dr. Hill described this experience with deep emotion: "My wife could have said, 'I never had this happen in the home I was raised in.'" But she didn't berate or blame him. Instead she said, "Somehow we'll get these lights back on, but tonight let's eat by candlelight."[9]

Our calling to love and respect is a calling regardless of what the other person does.

It's sacrificial. It's the script. And it works.

Now, here's the story of a divorce that didn't last because a couple learned to love one another as God wants all of us to.

An Example of Living by the Script

This was a testimony given before two thousand people in our congregation one morning:

Jim: I wondered why I was asked to give my testimony, and then I realized that the pastor knew that Marie and I were divorced and then remarried. I first thought the reason they asked me to share was that out of all the people in the congregation I had done the worst job the first time around in their marriage. But when we had the Forty Days of Purpose, one of the things I remembered from the book was when it talked about life as a metaphor. What immediately flashed in my mind is that it's a battle and a struggle. And it's always been a battle and struggle for me.

Marie and I were both living in Los Angeles in what most people would call the ghetto. We met when my mother worked with Marie's aunt. They wanted me to take her to her prom and I said no because I didn't have any fun at mine. Then I saw her picture and said yes. Eventually, in 1966, we were married.

I always believed in God, but I never let Him into my life, and I always tried to fight all the battles and struggles myself. I was a basketball coach and was focused on winning, winning, and winning. That's all I thought about. I brought all those struggles home and dumped them on her. Even though I was a leader at work, I really wasn't a leader at home. I just didn't know how to lead my family.

We were married twenty-three years before we got divorced in 1989, basically because I was such a poor leader. I did not give my wife the things she needed. I really didn't know exactly what those things were. We went through with the divorce and Marie went to Mexico City to study. I was a Christian at that time, but I wasn't walking with the Lord. But I prayed and asked Him to take over because I loved my wife and my family and I didn't want this situation. God was faithful to me and restored my marriage a year later. We were only divorced for one year.

I think the major things I have learned are that I can trust the Lord to fight my battles and that He will lead me if I give Him that opportunity. I think the major change in my life is that I am more of a spiritual leader in my home. I think I support my wife more now.

I know that women need to be loved, supported,

and cherished. As men, that's really the role God has given us—and He sets an example when He loves, supports, and cherishes His church. I'm trying to do a better job on that. I don't always do it, but the more that I can be in the Bible and listen to God speaking to me—because that's where He's speaking to me—and the more I can rely on Him, the more I can focus on my wife's positive gifts rather than on her negative traits and on trying to change her.

You see, that's what coaches do—we work on changing negative behavior so that we can get players to do the positive things so we can be successful. But I know I shouldn't carry that home—and that's what I did for years.

Marie is a very intelligent, compassionate, loving, and beautiful woman. We are very different. Last night, for example, she was reading her welding book and I was watching the De La Hoya fight. But we are meant to be together. The Scripture that I have relied on is 1 Peter 3:7, which says, "Live with your wives in an understanding way…and show them respect" [NCV].

Marie: I really like the cherish part. Jim was always a hardworking, responsible man. I never had to worry about any of the material things in our life, but I felt way down on his list of priorities. It seemed like basketball was number one, two, and three. He was very critical of me—whether it be my dress, my hair, or the smudge on the table. It didn't seem like I could do anything well, and the irony of it was that other people thought I did many things well. But none of that sank into my heart, because Jim was the one I wanted to please. My self-esteem was very wrapped up in what he thought of me.

My family had died. I was a young woman trying to raise a family—and without a foundation in the Lord. In fact, in our early marriage I was an atheist because of a lot of things that had happened to me. I was needy, and Jim wasn't able to show me the love he actually had for me.

I started to build up sadness and deep depression over the years, and after twenty-three years I thought, *I can't go on any longer like this.* But crying out to the Lord is an amazing thing. It wasn't an overnight change, but it turns out a church I was attending needed a singer and guitarist and I was pushed into the role. That's where I found out God was real, that Jesus Christ had died for my sins and that He was there for me.

Jim and I reaching out to the Lord has made such an incredible difference in our lives. Now Jim reads the Word faithfully, and I can see that he's devoted his life to God's plan. This has been a benefit to me and our family, because God's plan is that we be united. That has enriched our relationship.

Jim is now my biggest supporter. He helped me overcome my fear of going to school, so at the age of forty-four I went to college, got a bachelor's, master's, two teaching credentials, and two administrative credentials—when I thought I never could pass one college class.

And then last May Jim pushed me into doing a concert that was a magical experience—at an auditorium with more than six hundred people in attendance. I have found that I can rely upon my husband not just for material things, but for spiritual strength and for emotional support. Now he enumerates my strengths to me and to other people. He also helps me with my weaknesses, as a spouse should do, and in an uncritical way.

It's an amazing thing. In a short sentence: There is always hope in the Lord.

For Your Consideration

1. In what way(s) is this teaching a part of your marriage at this time? Describe it.

2. What could you do to implement this teaching in order to enhance your marriage? List specific steps.

Recommended Resources

Each for the Other, Bryan Chapell (Baker Books, 1998)

Love and Respect, Dr. Emerson Eggerichs (Integrity, 2004)

Communication: Key to Marriage, H. Norman Wright (Regal Books, 2001)

Chapter Five

COMMITMENT: THE SUPERGLUE OF MARRIAGE

OVER THE PAST one hundred years or so, our culture has rewritten the script of marriage a page at a time. When it comes to marriage, a permanence mentality has been replaced by one of exchange, one marriage forever by one marriage at a time.

There is a duality of thinking about marriage in our culture. On one hand, bridal magazines, fashions, wedding planners, and honeymoon spots are all big business. But a "If it doesn't work, bail out" attitude toward marriage undermines commitment, the very foundation of the institution.

These are not Marriage Keeper attitudes, are they?

The word that reflects God's script for marriage is *permanence*, meaning "lasting forever." This is strongly implied in the Bible's first reference to marriage: "For this reason a man shall leave his father and his mother, and be joined to his wife; and they shall become one flesh" (Genesis 2:24, NASB).

In this context, the word *joined* doesn't refer to something that can be separated, such as two railroad cars that can be coupled but later easily separated. On the contrary, the Hebrew word for *joined* means "to adhere," "to cling," "to cleave," or "to stick." It implies a lasting bond and one marriage for life. Jesus quoted this same passage in the Gospel of Matthew, and the Greek word used there means "to be glued together." In this context, that word doesn't speak of confinement but of a permanent bond and an unleashing of potential.

Divorce: Not an Option

You've probably heard of the old military expression, "Surrender is not an option." When a ship's captain headed into battle—where surrender definitely wasn't an option—he would give the order to nail his country's colors to the mast. After the flags were nailed up high, during battle there was just no way to lower them and run up the flag of surrender. When the crew realized there was no option but to fight, they became more determined to win the battle.

This is the same mindset we're to have in marriage. Our one option in marriage is to stand our ground, fight off the things that would separate us from one another, and find a way make it work.

Can you imagine what would happen if the attorneys, judges, ministers, and friends of couples wanting out of their marriages told them, "There is no 'out'—no divorce. Go back and work it out. Change yourselves and rekindle your love. That's your only option"?

I believe if we understood the level of commitment God requires of us in marriage, we would do anything and everything we could not just to make our marriages survive, but to make them successful. You see, a Christian marriage goes beyond an earthly partnership. It's a commitment involving three individuals—the husband, the wife, and Jesus Christ.

King Solomon wrote, "One standing alone can be attacked and defeated, but two can stand back-to-back and conquer; three is even better, for a triple-braided cord is not easily broken" (Ecclesiastes 4:12, TLB). In the context of marriage, that means that with the husband and wife committed to one another and to Jesus, they have the tools at their disposal to make their marriage a successful one.

Commitment means many things to different people. For some, the strength of their commitment is only as strong as they feel emotionally or physically. That can be a shaky foundation.

Real commitment is not based on feelings but on the vows we make before God and other people when we get married. It is a promise and a pledge we carry out to completion—running over any roadblocks that get in the way. Marriage is a total giving of oneself to another person. Of course, that kind of commitment is risky, but it makes life more fulfilling.

I have compared the idea of commitment in marriage to bungee jumping. In that particular activity, once you take the plunge off the platform, there is no turning back and no changing your mind; you're committed to following through with the jump.

That's what a commitment looks like, and it's what holds a marriage together, even when times get tough.

The Strength of a Promise

In Thornton Wilder's "The Skin of Our Teeth," a character named Ms. Antobus says, "I married you because you gave me a promise. That promise made up for your faults. And the promise I gave you made up for mine. Two imperfect people got married and it was the promise that made the marriage.... And when our children were growing up, it wasn't a house that protected them; and it wasn't our love that protected them—it was that promise."[1]

That's a great example of what a commitment to marriage looks like. It's a promise made and kept by two imperfect people—people with flaws, faults, and character weaknesses.

Commitment means relinquishing the childish dream of having a spouse who gratifies all of your needs and desires and who makes up for all your childhood disappointments. It means expecting and accepting the fact that your spouse will disappoint you and at times not live up to your expectations. And it means sticking with your spouse when difficulties come your way in the marriage, which they eventually will.

A friend of mine once told me how it was the commitment to his marriage that made it last: "Norm, we each had a commitment to each other and to the marriage. When our commitment to each other was low, it was the commitment to the marriage that kept us together."

Marital commitment means looking to ourselves first when

ONE MARRIAGE UNDER GOD

difficulties arise. It is human nature to look at everything and everyone but ourselves when we're going through tough times. We look at our spouse, at other people, at marriage itself. Down the line, we may or may not get around to pointing the finger of blame at ourselves.

A person of commitment does the opposite because he or she knows that marriage is not a prison but a source of freedom and security. For that reason, the person of commitment looks to himself first and asks, "How am I contributing to this problem?" People of commitment know that they can control only their own behavior and thoughts, and not those of their spouse.[2]

Committed to Loving Well

Most people when they first marry have no idea the kind of pain that can accompany the commitment to live together for life. They don't understand that they are binding themselves together with another human being—legally, economically, physically, emotionally, and spiritually.

Each of us will suffer at different points in our lives, and when we are married, we are committed to sharing in the pain of another person. For that reason, we need to look to our commitment and to their marriage vows for strength, stability, and endurance—especially when feelings of love aren't as strong as they once were.

This means regularly remembering to take the time to express our love and commitment to one another and to say the things that need to be said and need to be heard in a loving, committed marriage.

In short, it's a commitment to love well.

Read the words of one wife:

Real-life death scenes aren't like the movies. My husband, too tall for a regulation bed, lay with his feet sticking out of the covers. I stood clinging to his toes as though that would save his life. I clung so that if I failed to save him from falling off the cliff of the present, of the here and now, we'd go together. That's how it was in the netherworld of the intensive care unit....

It seemed that the entire world had turned into night. Cold and black. No place you'd volunteer to enter. Doctors tried to be kind. Their eyes said, *This is out of our hands. There's nothing more we can do.*

A nurse with a soft Jamaican lilt placed a pink blanket over my shoulders. Someone whispered, "It's just a matter of minutes."

Just a matter of minutes to tell each other anything we had forgotten to say. Just a few minutes to take an accounting of our days together. Had we loved well enough?[3]

This wife's question calls each of us back to our marriage commitment. No matter whether we've been married a few months, a few years, or several decades, it causes us to look at our spouse and our marriage and ask ourselves, "Have I loved well enough?"

What about you? Are you "up-to-date"? Have you taken the time to put into words the things you need and want to say and the things your spouse needs and wants to hear? If you haven't, it's not too late to do a little catching up.

Myself, I sometimes reflect on past thoughts and feelings I wish I had verbalized. But I've realized that it's all right to go to my wife and remind her of a situation or conversation we once went though and tell her what I wish I had said at the time.

I try to stay on the alert so that I can remain up-to-date and catch those moments and take the time to say the things I know I'll wish I'd said later.

For example, our pastor and his wife recently stopped by with a plant and an offer to pray for Joyce, who had an upcoming visit to the doctor. When the pastor began praying for Joyce, there came over her face a beautiful expression of sweetness, innocence, and peace. At that moment, I wished I had a camera so I could capture that expression someplace other than in my mind. Later, however, I shared this with Joyce. I told her what I was feeling and thinking as I saw the look on her face as our pastor prayed for her. Just talking to Joyce about that moment was an expression of my love and commitment for her, an expression that deepened my love and commitment all the more.

A commitment to love well is not restricted to those times when all of life's puzzle pieces—or those of the marriage itself—fall perfectly into place. It's not contingent on our circumstances, but a commitment to endure everything life throws our way.

In marriage, you may have a day that goes perfectly now and then, but you'll have many days that won't. But every day, no matter how it goes, we need to take the time to ask ourselves if we've loved well enough.

If we have, then we can rejoice and remember those days for the rest of our marriage. But if we haven't, we can begin now. It's never too late to start loving well.

A Commitment to Be on Your Guard

In the early- to mid-1980s, the action-packed television show *Hill Street Blues* captivated viewers. Part of what made the show such a hit was the motley group of characters who occupied the offices at this precinct. Some of them weren't exactly the kind of officers you'd want to show up if you ever needed help!

Each episode of *Hill Street Blues* began with a morning—and often chaotic—briefing of all the officers. Just before the sergeant dismissed the rowdy group, he would pause and say, "Let's be careful out there!" This was his warning to be on the alert, keep their guard up, and never slack off, because the unpredictable could and often would happen.

Scripture warns us again and again to "be on your guard." Be on your guard, Jesus said, against hypocrisy (see Matthew 16:6–12); against greed (see Luke 12:15); against persecution from others (see Matthew 10:17); against false teaching (see Mark 13:22–23); and above all, against spiritual slackness and unreadiness for the Lord's return (see Mark 13:32–37). "Be careful," Jesus said in Luke 21:34, "or your hearts will be weighed down with dissipation, drunkenness and the anxieties of life."

Being careful in this context means to be wary, to keep your eyes open, to be alert, because if you let down your guard, you may do something to harm yourself or others. That is why the same caution is repeated throughout the Scriptures. Listen to these warnings: "Only be careful, and watch yourselves" (Deuteronomy 4:9); "Be careful to do what the LORD your God has commanded you" (Deuteronomy 5:32); "Be careful to obey all that is written in the Book" (Joshua 23:6); "Give careful thought to your ways" (Haggai 1:5–7); "Be careful to do what is right" (Romans 12:17); "Be careful that you don't fall" (1 Corinthians 10:12); "Be very careful, then, how you live" (Ephesians 5:15); and "Be careful that none of you be found to have fallen short" (Hebrews 4:1).

God gives us these warnings to be careful because He knows that in order to endure what the world is throwing at us, we need to be wary and cautious. That applies to our marriage commitment.

Many people don't see the word *endurance* in a positive way, mostly because they tend to associate it with the hard work it takes to get through difficult times. While the idea of a commitment to endure may not seem romantic or inspiring, it actually has a liberating, strengthening effect within a marriage. Within a marriage, this type of commitment helps genuine intimacy develop and flourish. That's because a commitment to endure even the most difficult of circumstances can make marriage a place of refuge and encouragement.

As Christians, this commitment to endure ultimately originates in our confidence in God's character. It involves the recognition that God will not allow the heaviness of life's circumstances to outweigh or overwhelm the encouragement He gives us. It's built on the assurance that He can and will guide couples through even the most difficult predicaments they face.

One wife shared her thoughts:

We have been married fifty years, so you can just imagine how much change we have gone through: three wars, eleven presidents, five recessions, going from the Model A to the moon and from country roads to the information superhighway. While these changes around us have been great, the personal changes that God has enacted within us through each other have been even greater. Although we often couldn't see how God was working in our lives at the time, we look back now and realize that our marriage has been a school of character development. God has used my husband in my life, and me in his, to make us more like Christ. So what are the lessons that we've learned about how God uses marriage to change us? There are many. Through fifty years of marriage we've learned that differences develop us, that crises cultivate us, and that ministry melts us together.

This is a couple who not only endured but who flourished, simply because they had a commitment to love one another and to be on guard against the things the devil could have used to damage their marriage.

A "Two-Tiered" Commitment

For a Christian marriage to be stable and to grow, the couple must have a commitment to both marriage as an *institution* and marriage as a *relationship*. Commitment to the institution of marriage creates a context in which growth can take place, while commitment to a marriage relationship guarantees that those things that are to constitute an individual marriage will take place. Together, these two commitments create a marrage.[4]

I believe it's important to review this "two-tiered" commitment and to "recreate" the marriage commitment every day. It takes more than celebrating an anniversary once a year, or even once a month. It takes more than a weekly "date night." It is important to recreate your commitment every single day you are married.

When I say we should "recreate" our commitment, I mean that we simply do the things it takes to remind ourselves of our commitment. And how do we do that? Here's one example I've taken from my own devotional life:

Each morning during my devotional time I take out a stack of three-by-five-inch index cards, on which I've written passages of Scripture I'm memorizing, and I review them. Also, sometimes when I wake up at night, I run some of these Scriptures through my mind and reflect on them in order to help me memorize them.

It has occurred to me that the same thing might work when it comes to "recreating" my marriage commitment every day. I'm talking about simply taking a three-by-five card every morning and writing on it a reminder of my commitment to marriage as an institution as well as my marriage relationship with my wife.

Reminders of your commitment to marriage itself and to *your* marriage in particular can be very helpful when it comes to "recreating" your marriage daily. And it's something I encourage when I conduct premarital counseling.

When I work with couples who are planning to marry, I ask each of them to write out twelve specific reasons they want to marry the other person, then during one of the sessions I ask them to face one another and read those reasons aloud. Some of these experiences have been deeply moving, even to the point of bringing all three of us to tears.

After a couple reads their list to one another I suggest two things: First, that they post this list in their home to serve as a reminder of why they are making this commitment to one another; and second, that they make it an anniversary tradition to read their list aloud, then to add reasons they're happy they married one another that they've discovered over the previous year.

Can you recall your reasons for marrying your spouse? Can you think of things you've learned about your partner over the past year or five years or ten years you've been married that make you glad you made the commitment you did?

If you've not reflected on these questions, or if you've never written down the reasons you're happy to be married to your spouse, take the time to do so now. It will make a difference in the way you see your commitment to marriage as an institution and to *your* marriage as a relationship.

Keeping the Commitment Strong:
A Matter of Focus

So, what works in keeping commitment strong? What can you do to protect your promise? Think about this.

Two problems that can lead to the erosion of commitment are overestimation and underestimation. Now, sometimes overestimation can be a good thing. For example, most of us would be pleased if a contractor gave us a bid on home improvements, then told us after the work was done that the job cost less than he thought it would. On the other hand, underestimation would be a bad thing if that same contractor underbid the job but informed us later it cost more than he originally said.

I have found in my years as a counselor that both overestimation and underestimation can cause difficulties in a marriage. How does that happen? Here are some examples.

It's very easy to underestimate the level of satisfaction in a marriage, while at the same time overestimating the number of problems in the relationship. When this happens, it's very often caused by a distortion of what is actually going on in the relationship. The results, as you might expect, can be very painful.

Usually, this distorted view of a couple's relationship—by one or both partners—happens because they are very much like mules with blinders on. If you've not seen blinders on a horse or mule, let me explain what they are. Blinders keep the animal from seeing what's going on around them. They can see directly ahead of them, but they have no peripheral vision.

We can be very much like animals with blinders on in that we often get focused on what we think we lack while not seeing all the good things going on around us. But this is a correctable situation.

We get an accurate view of our marriage when we simply remove the blinders so we can change the direction we're going. Once the blinders are lifted, we need only reverse what we've been doing. Focus on the positives in your marriage—what *is* working in your marriage—and not on the negatives.

Cutting Your Spouse Some Slack

As Christians we're called to give our spouses the benefit of the doubt, or, as the phrase goes, to "cut our spouse some slack."

You can start doing this by simply refusing to assume the worst when your spouse does something out of the ordinary. When that happens, don't assume that your spouse has ulterior motives or is angry or upset with you. Instead, start with the assumption of good intentions. When you do that, your spouse is more likely to live up to those assumptions.

The phrase "cut them some slack" comes from fishing. I saw an example of that one day as I was bass fishing over some sunken trees. As I was retrieving my lure after one cast, a very large bass took my lure and proceeded to strip line from my reel. I did my best to turn the fish before it plowed deeper into the underwater trees, but he managed to wrap himself and the line around a tree trunk.

I saw the fish for just a second before he went deep, and I knew he was a big one. I wanted to land this fish, and I had a couple of options. I could engage in a tug-o'-war with the fish—pull harder on the line and attempt to pull him out of the underwater stump. This seemed like the obvious choice—simply engage the fish in a power struggle and show him I'm in charge. But I knew from experience that this would backfire; all it would accomplish was rubbing the line against the stump until it frayed and broke. That way, I'd lose not only the fish but also the lure he had in his mouth.

My other option, which didn't feel totally comfortable to me, was to take the pressure off the fish, give him some slack in the line, and let him have the freedom to swim around on his own. Then perhaps he'd unwrap himself and swim out away from the stump. This meant giving up some control and letting him do what he wanted for a while. This was going to take patience. If this were to work, it would be on his terms and in his own time.

So I cut the fish some slack, then waited. Slowly, the line began to move, and when the fish swam out from the stump I was ready. After a few minutes of struggle, I landed him, took a picture, and released him to grow even larger.

Later, I realized how the way I handled that fish is so much like many of us need to learn to handle our spouses. Just as I gave that big bass some slack and he came my way, when we cut our spouses some slack, they also come our way. Couples who follow this principle rather than trying to confine and control one another discover a higher level of satisfaction in their marriages.

A Commitment to the Right Priority

In Stephen Covey's book *First Things First*, he illustrates the importance of committing ourselves to the right priorities with the following story:

> At a time management seminar, the speaker set a large jar on a table in front of the attendees, then placed several softball-size rocks around it. He asked the crowd, "How many of these rocks do you think I can fit into

this jar? The guesses begin. Thirteen! Nine! Twelve! After several guesses had been called out, he began to place the rocks, one at a time, into the jar. As he did this he counted out loud: One, two, three, and so on. After placing each rock in the jar, he asked the participants if the jar was full. They kept answering no until the twelfth rock was in the jar, at which point it appeared full.

With the jar apparently filled with rocks, the speaker brought out a bucketful of smaller rocks and began pouring them into the jar. The smaller stones slid around the larger ones, filling in the gaps, until the jar was again apparently full. At that point, the speaker asked the crowd, "Is the jar full yet?" to which they responded, "No!"

By now the crowd knew what was coming next: sand and then water. Only then was the jar full.

With the jar now truly full, the seminar leader asked, "What's the point of this?" to which one seminar attendee answered, "The point is that there are all these nooks and crannies and places of time in life that we are just wasting and not using to the fullest."

"No," the seminar leader said, "that's not the point." He then pointed out that if the big rocks hadn't gone into the jar first, they wouldn't have made it into the jar at all.

"It's about setting apart time," he said. "You have a jar. So do I. Most of our jars are full. It's impossible to create more time, so it's a limited resource. So what are the big rocks? Those are the things you believe are most important in your life. I wonder how often we go through life with some of the most important big rocks not in the jar but sitting on the table. A big rock is an intended priority, but if it's not in the jar, it's not an actual priority."[5]

Commitment means making sure you get your spouse in the jar first. Most of us would say that our spouse is one of the big rocks, but are they really? When we make our spouse one of the "big rocks" in the jar of our lives, we set ourselves up for marital happiness and fulfillment.

Commitment means saying yes to time with your spouse and no to many other things. Dr. Scott Stanley wrote, "Commitment involves making the choice to give up some choices. Further, really sticking with your commitment will require a person to protect the choice they have made in the context of life's demands. Keeping commitments requires all of us to recognize that some paths are no longer available to us. We have to give them up."[6]

Finally, each of us needs to make a commitment to commitment itself. At first that sounds like a strange challenge, but it's simply the belief and the conviction that we will finish what we start, especially when it comes to our marriages.

For Your Consideration

1. What are the choices you have given up?
2. What are the paths you have given up?
3. How are you protecting your choice of commitment?
4. Ask yourself again, *What is it like being married to*

me?

Chapter Six

WE'VE BEEN
FOOLED

YEARS AGO, an old television commercial for a particular brand of margarine featured the line, "It's not *nice* to fool Mother Nature." The joke behind the commercial was that the margarine tasted so much like real butter that even Mother Nature herself couldn't tell the difference.

That was a fairly amusing commercial, but in truth we know that it's not nice to fool anyone, particularly when they don't find out until much later that they've been fooled.

In our culture today, all kinds of efforts are made to fool consumers. Ads promise us "incredible savings" on credit cards, cars, furniture, and anything else we can find to spend money on, but there's always an "oh, by the way" hitch attached. It always turns out that we weren't given all the information up front, and that what the ad initially told us wasn't completely truthful.

If you've ever fallen for a less than truthful ad on television or on the radio, you probably felt not only let down but betrayed—"fooled," as the old commercial put it.

It's bad when an individual or group receives and believes false information, and it's worse when a community is misled. But it's downright tragic when an entire culture is misled to believe what isn't true. When that happens, there is an erosion of values, beliefs, and trust.

That's exactly what has happened to our culture when it comes to the institution of marriage. We have been fed the line that cohabitation, or "living together" outside of marriage is the same as marriage itself, that it is an answer to the problem of divorce or unhappy marriage.

Sadly, many people in our culture—including some Bible-believing Christians—have been fooled by this lie. You may have experienced this firsthand—and if not, you no doubt have friends and relatives who have. If either of these scenarios is true for you, then you probably realize it's time to speak out against the myth that living together has advantages over marriage and time to let people know that this is nothing more than a rewrite of God's script for marriage.

Marriage is under attack by the trend of cohabitation— and this applies in the Christian community also. The problem, I believe, isn't that the church hasn't spoken out on this issue. In fact, many churches still strongly encourage couples to live apart and abstain from a sexual relationship until they marry.

I believe the problem is more that Christian couples have not spoken out or presented marriage as a positive lifestyle for people today. We'll get to that later, but for now, let's take a look at the state of cohabitation in our culture today.

The Numbers and the Rationales for Cohabitation

Cohabitation is a practice that has increased dramatically in our culture over the past three decades. We are not-so-slowly moving from being a "marriage culture" to a "cohabitation culture." The numbers don't lie. In 1970, around half a million couples were living together in the United States, but by the year 2000 the number had risen to around 5.5 million.[1]

This trend of unmarried cohabitation is on the rise, and it cuts across all cultural and religious lines. People of all religious faiths—even those whose beliefs explicitly forbid unmarried cohabitation—are living together. Some pastors are reporting that 30 to 50 percent of the couples coming to them for marriage are living together.

Couples who live together offer any number of reasons for it. For some, it's a matter of finances or economics. They argue that if they live together, they can pool their resources, split expenses, and save money—basically, that they can afford a higher standard of living than if they lived alone. Others live together for tax or inheritance reasons. For example, some unmarried senior citizens cohabitate rather than marry because they would lose income if they chose to marry.

Many people live together unmarried simply because they are lonely and want companionship. They don't want the legal ties of being married (or they believe that marriage as we once knew it has run its course and is irrelevant today), but they don't like living alone either. So in order to fulfill their emotional and sexual needs, they move in together. Also, the fear of losing their companion has created pressure for some to cohabit.[2]

While those who live together outside of marriage may or may not plan to marry or have children, for many living together is their way of seeing of they are "compatible" enough to marry. To them, it's a matter of "taking the risk out of marriage." (More on that myth later.)

One young man—I'll call him Jim—told me, "My parents divorced and so did Jill's. Neither of us wants that for ourselves. So we think of living together like a shakedown cruise for a new ship. We want to get all the bugs out before we go into service."

Many people who choose to live together have already decided that they will be married and figure that they don't need to make things "legal" before they move in together. "We love each other so much. We are going to get married someday anyway, so why wait?" said one young woman. In truth, the majority of couples who live together *are* planning to marry sometime in the future.[3]

So what would you say to someone—a friend, coworker, neighbor, relative, or even one of your own children—who announces that he or she is planning to move in and live with someone out of marriage? If that hasn't happened to you yet, it very likely will in the future.

When that happens, you may feel put on the spot and struggle with a response. But if you start with some nonjudgmental, practical arguments against cohabitating, you just might get that person's attention.

Here are some good arguments *against* cohabitation.

Cohabitation: A Failed Experiment

Unmarried cohabitation is a great social experiment which research has shown us very clearly has failed miserably. While it has been touted as a healthy alternative to marriage, in that respect it just hasn't measured up.

The idea that living together can be a selection process—like trying on a new outfit or pair of shoes—for marriage is a treacherous one. That is because human relationships are not like clothing, where you simply try them on and decide if the cuffs are too long or the hem too short.

The lure of cohabitation is that it is a relationship without strings, one that people can enter or leave with ease. However, unacknowledged strings can bind very tightly.

Part of the difficulty in living together is it doesn't demand equal responsibility from each person. It can lead to unrealistic rescue fantasies and dependency on the part of one or both who may be trying to escape from an unhappy past. It's quite easy to slip into living together—no real commitment, no trying to please family members—but it doesn't guarantee that the ending will be easy.[4]

But this only scratches the surface of the problems living together poses for those who choose that path.

First, the published research over the past few decades has shown that cohabitation doesn't even produce the desired results when it comes to lowering a couple's odds of divorcing. Several studies have shown very clearly that living together does not decrease the risk of divorce but actually *increases* it. The statistics tell us that three out of four couples—75 percent—who live together before marrying end up getting divorced.[5]

Second, it has been shown that there is a higher risk of emotional and physical abuse between couples who live together outside of marriage. In fact, this kind of aggression is almost twice as common among these couples as it is among those who are married. According to the U.S. Justice Department, a woman is much more likely to be assaulted if living with a man than if she was married.[6]

The third major problem with living together is that those who do have measurably lower levels of happiness than those couples who marry. This includes higher levels of depression and anxiety. The lack of commitment—the kind found only in marriage—helps create this situation. Adding to that is the higher level of unfaithfulness among those who live together outside of marriage.[7]

Not surprisingly, this unhappiness and unfaithfulness often follows the couple into marriage, should it go that far. Both partners are less likely to be as happy and sexually satisfied as a married couple. Furthermore, women who live with men before marriage are more likely to be unfaithful once married than women who don't.

Then there is the issue of living together being a "warm-up" for marriage. The truth is that only about 60 percent of those who live together end up marrying one another.[8]

You can see already that the "cohabitation experiment" our culture has been going through has been a major failure on many levels. But we're not finished yet.

As we pointed out earlier, one of the reasons many couples live together is so they can split expenses and live more cheaply.

ONE MARRIAGE UNDER GOD

But the studies have shown that unlike marriage, in which couples tend to hold joint accounts, most couples who live together keep their banking accounts separate, even taking steps to keep their time and money separate. Furthermore, they may intend to split everything fifty-fifty, but women more often then not tend to contribute the most financially to the arrangement—often as much as 70 percent.[9]

One of the final arguments against cohabitation is that in many areas of life, the couple and their arrangement will not be accepted the same way as those who are married. In short, they will be treated and addressed differently from those who are married.

The aftermath of 9/11 offered many tragic examples of the realities of what may be referred to as the "live-in" relationship. Many married people lost their spouses in the tragic collapse of the towers, and they were recognized. Their spouses were honored and financial payments were made. Not so with many of those who were living together. In a sense, many of them were on their own in their loss, their grief, and their financial responsibilities.

Living together outside of marriage may appear to provide short-term benefits, but they come at a long-term cost. Couples who choose to cohabitate lose many of the benefits of marriage while weakening the possibility of success if they do marry.[10]

When a couple takes that step of commitment called marriage, they open doors for themselves that would otherwise be closed to those who are single or living together. One of the reasons is that when you marry, you do so believing that your relationship will last until one of you dies.

This helps you to feel freer to invest your life with someone else than if you were just living together. You're freer to develop a compatible working relationship. Because of the "permanence" belief that each is committed to the other, each person can develop their potential and skills to complement one another and work as a team.

Daring to Speak Up

This growing trend of cohabitation instead of marriage is more than just an alternative to the marriage commitment; it is an absolute attack on the institution of marriage as we know it, and we as Christians and as Marriage Keepers need to respond.

The questions you need to ask yourself are, With whom will you share this information? Who in your circle of friends or relatives needs to know of the risks and dangers of living together outside of marriage? Can you share this information with young people in your church, youth group, or community in general? And if not, why not?

Keep in mind that the information I've just laid out for you is best received by someone who personally knows the person sharing it. Our churches could share this information in detail from the pulpit (many do) or distribute the information to every attendee. But the pastoral staff of your local church can't do it all. This means that you may be called upon to confront someone with this information.

When you are faced with responding to someone's

announcement that he or she is about to move in with a member of the opposite sex without taking the step of getting married, you should have a response. By all means listen, because listening opens others to what you have to say. But also be ready to speak up when the time comes.

Right about now, you may be thinking that you don't have it in you to say what needs to be said in such a situation, that it's not your responsibility, that you don't want to offend someone by being confrontational. However, as Christians—and as Marriage Keepers—it is our responsibility to help and guide others, even if it means confronting them with the fact that they are making a mistake. That is especially true when the person or persons in question are believers. As the apostle Paul wrote, "Brothers, if someone is caught in a sin, you who are spiritual should restore him gently. But watch yourself, or you also may be tempted" (Galatians 6:1).

When you need to confront someone about anything, the way or manner in which you do it is of paramount importance. If your attitude is judgmental or condemning, your words will be met with resistance or worse. This is especially true in situations like the one we're discussing here.

If you are faced with this kind of situation right now, ask yourself what you have to lose by confronting the ones who are considering making the mistake of living together outside of marriage, then ask yourself what you (or they) have to gain. I would be willing to bet that there is a lot more to be gained than lost in this situation.

What could you say to a couple who is living together or is about to?

"I appreciate your telling me about your situation. It sounds as though if you do marry, you want it to work. We all do. Have you ever heard of the book *Great Expectations*? Well, if a book were written about couples living together, it could be titled *Great Expectations—Surprising Results*. Would you be interested in hearing what these result are? I was shocked when I first heard them. The *Reader's Digest* condensed version is this: All the research on couples living together shows that instead of reducing the risk of divorce, it actually increases it by 50 percent; instead of reducing conflict and aggression, it increases it by 50 percent; instead of moving toward marriage, the chances of not marrying are 40 to 50 percent greater. All in all, it elevates the risk factor. As someone said, would you want to parachute from an airplane if you knew that one out of every two chutes would fail? If I were hearing this for the first time, I'd tend to think, *Well, we're an exception to that.* Perhaps. But then again... If you're interested in learning more about this, you may want to read the book *Before You Live Together* by David Gudgel. Thanks for considering what I've said."

Do you have anything to lose by sharing this? Not really. Do you have anything to gain? I don't know, but you may have helped a couple change the direction of their life. And you've responded as a Marriage Keeper.

For Your Consideration

1. Describe what you will do with the information in this chapter.
2. Who do you know that is living together that you could begin praying for?

Chapter Seven

DIVORCE: NOT A GOOD ALTERNATIVE

REMEMBER THE ANGUISHED, despairing words of your friend in chapter 1? If not, here's exactly what she said: "It's over. I haven't been happy in this marriage for years. Why stay and be miserable? Nothing seems to make a change! We're all miserable, so at least divorce will give both of us a fresh start and a chance at finding a soul mate. And the kids are resilient. They can adjust. I just need some people in my corner to support me right now."

As a marriage counselor, I've heard cries of desperation and hopelessness such as these again and again. Perhaps you've heard words like these yourself—or had similar thoughts or feelings of your own.

When you come to the end of your rope, it becomes easier and easier to say "I've had it" or "It's over."

Let's look closely at what the desperate woman at the beginning of chapter 1 said:

"I haven't been happy in my marriage…."

"I'm miserable…."

"Nothing seems to make a change…."

"It's always going to be this way…."

"Divorce will give us a fresh start…."

"The children will be all right…."

Do you see the progression of thought? Unhappiness followed by misery, followed by the feeling that nothing will change, followed by the solution. For someone in that situation, divorce seems like the answer. After all, both people are miserable and would be better off apart. Besides, it won't affect the kids.

When someone is in this frame of mind, they usually look for a friend or acquaintance to support them in their decision to get out of their marriage. Knowing that, if you were to receive a phone call like this one, what would be your response?

You have numerous options, including:

- Silence.
- "I don't know what to say. Have you talked to a counselor?"
- "Well, if you've tried and there's no change, then why be miserable?"
- "There are no biblical grounds for you to divorce, so you can't divorce."

- "It's too bad the marriage isn't working, but there is probably someone out there who could make you happy."
- "Well, you're not alone. Look at all the others at church who are divorced."

What *would* you say if a friend told you of his or her impending divorce? Most of us struggle with that kind of situation. We want to help our friends, but we want to do it without condoning what they're doing. We'd like to offer alternatives to divorce, but we're afraid to offend or alienate anyone. Or maybe we're just afraid of becoming too involved or of appearing to take sides in the divorce.

The caller above, like so many others, has shelved God's plan for marital perseverance in the quest for someone else to make her happy. What she fails to see, however, is that divorce doesn't affect just her and her husband but also has a ripple effect that spreads through the neighborhood, the school, the church, and, yes, through society.

Like cohabitation, divorce has failed to deliver on its promises of happiness.

Divorce always creates hardships on the husband and wife, but also on the children and other relatives. It's like a tearing of a fabric that leaves harsh lines and ragged threads.

Most people who divorce fail to work through the issues as well as grief that divorce brings, which usually takes two to three years. Consequently, those who divorce usually make one of two additional mistakes. They either marry a person who is similar to the first spouse—often re-creating the very same problems in the first marriage—or they go out of their way to marry some-one totally different without working on themselves.

Sadly, neither of these approaches has a high success rate, and the rate of divorce for second and third marriages is statistically higher than for first marriages.

Preventing Divorce

The question we need to ask—as individuals, as couples, and as church bodies—is, *What are we doing to prevent divorce or to intervene in the lives of those seeking divorce?*

It's easy to look at the problem of divorce—its causes and effects—then simply say of those on the brink of divorce, "Let's pray for them." But this is an issue that needs more than prayer; it needs intervention on the part of godly people.

In order to bring marriage back to the prominent place God has for it in our world, we need couples who will be what I call "interventionist healers." This is part of being a Marriage Keeper. We also need for our country to begin seeking marriage—marriage between one man and one woman—as *the* option, not cohabitation, not divorce. One way we as couples can begin to accomplish this is by making sure that our marriages are role models for our culture and the next generation.

Ask yourself, *Does my marriage qualify as a role model?* What can you begin doing to have it stand out in a way that would make others around you see your marriage and want to emulate it? Are you praying and thinking about ways you can do these things?

The sooner we realize we're called to be examples in our

marriages, the sooner we will begin working harder at following God's' script and seeing our marriages grow in new ways.

When a husband and wife divorce, there will always be fall-out and damage in the lives of others around them, and those who suffer most are, as you might expect, the children.

The Effects of Divorce on Children

We are now living in a time when approximately 45 percent of all children in the United States will live with only one parent before they reach the age of eighteen. Twelve million children in that age group now have parents who are divorced. At the rate we are going, we could see a time when the *majority* of our children could be from families whose parents are divorced. It has been estimated that by the year 2008, the traditional notion of family—one mom and one dad with children—will be replaced by the stepfamily.

The effects of divorce on children can be devastating, as the authors of the book *The Unexpected Legacy of Divorce* point out:

> Divorce is a life-transforming experience. After divorce, childhood is different. Adolescence is different. Adulthood—with the decision to marry or not and have children or not—is different....
>
> From the viewpoint of the children, and counter to what happens to their parents, divorce is a cumulative experience. Its impact increases over time and rises to a crescendo in adulthood. In adulthood it

affects personality, the ability to trust, expectations about relationships, and ability to cope with change.

The first upheaval occurs at the breakup. Children are frightened and angry, terrified of being abandoned by both parents, and they feel responsible for the divorce. Most children are taken by surprise; few are relieved....

As the postdivorce family took shape, their world increasingly resembled what they feared most. Home was a lonely place. The household was in disarray for years. Many children were forced to move, leaving behind familiar schools, close friends, and other supports....

As the children told us, adolescence begins early in divorced homes and, compared with that of youngsters raised in intact families, is more likely to include more early sexual experiences for girls and higher alcohol and drug use for girls and boys. Adolescence is more prolonged in divorced families and extends well into the years of early adulthood....

But it's in adulthood that children of divorce suffer the most. The impact of divorce hits them most cruelly as they go in search of love, sexual intimacy, and commitment.[1]

Amazingly, many parents don't believe that divorce damages children. They come to that conclusion because they know of divorced parents who have children that are well-balanced and successful. It's true that many children of divorced parents do well in school, life, marriage, and parenting. They are overcomers, which we as believers are all called to be. The presence of Jesus Christ in their lives and their commitment to Him as Lord has helped make up for what they lost when their parents split up. But the truth of the matter—and I've seen this many, many times—is that even those children of divorce who succeed in life started out at a disadvantage and had to work harder to overcome that disadvantage.

Don't believe it? Read on!

The vast majority of children don't want their parents to divorce. Most children who go through their parents' divorce are like bystanders caught in a flood, swept away by the current, and losing much of what they know as life. A child caught in a divorce suffers multiple losses. These can include not only the loss of one of the parents but also the loss of a home, neighborhood, school friends, and standard of living, as well as family outings, holiday get-togethers, and other activities.

Other losses might include:

- The loss of the expectation that the child's family will be together forever.
- The loss of trust: "If I can't depend on my parents, who can I depend on?"
- The loss of the familiar, the routine, and the safe.
- The possible loss of frequent access to a set of grandparents as well as the addition of a new set (with a remarriage).

There is one other even more devastating loss many children of divorce suffer: the loss of *both* parents, at least in the emotional sense. Studies have shown that the distress of a divorce, coupled with the daily demands of being a single parent, can make a mother and father less available to their children, both physically and emotionally. In that situation, both parents tend to be less emotionally responsive to their children.[2]

When a child's parents divorce, he or she is thrust into experiencing ongoing and repeated losses as well as feelings of rejection. Even the process of divorce itself is damaging to a child, who often suffers though the "revolving door" of repeated separations as a parent moves out and then returns. And when a child understands the parents have finally decided to divorce, it fuels those feelings of rejection. Later, the child may struggle to develop relationships with a new stepparent as well as new stepsiblings.[3]

When a child loses the stability of a two-parent home, he or she may lose hope for the future. An uncertainty worms its way into the child's mind; the child can feel more out of control than ever before. The stability of the two-parent home on which the child depended is no longer there for the child.

As you can see, it's folly to believe that children are resilient and that divorce won't affect them. Those who divorce may be looking for happiness—for a fresh start and a new life—but in seeking it that way, they are damaging their children and setting them up for failure in life. Obviously, living in a home with two married parents—God's plan for the family—is by far the best option for any child growing up.

A child raised in a single-parent household is more likely to have less money available to him or her. This causes the average child's standard of living to drop by about one-third. This is especially true when the father, who has promised to take care of the family through his monthly payments, doesn't make the payments on time or fails to make them at all.

But the child loses more than financial support when a divorce happens. Divorce decreases the amount of time a child can spend with each parent. By contrast, in an intact home with two parents, there are twice as many hours available to give the children.[4]

On average, children of divorce have more health disorders—both physical and psychological. Some of this is as a result of the emotional struggles of the parents, many of whom suffer anxiety and depression during a divorce. This adversely affects their ability to parent, and since children tend to draw stability from the parents, if it's not available a child also suffers.[5]

Another factor when it comes to the children's health is that divorced parents tend to have less money and more difficulty paying for health insurance, which can affect their children's health. One study indicated that divorce made it 50 percent more likely a child would have health problems.[6]

The effects of divorce on a child's health are not just immediate, but long-term as well. It has been shown that people from broken homes have a life expectancy four years shorter than those from homes where the parents stayed married. Forty-year-olds from divorced homes were three times more likely to die from various health causes than forty-year-olds whose parents stayed married.[7]

Children also suffer relationally from their parents' breakup, largely because of the conflicts, arguments, and other negative examples relating to divorce. The lack of effective conflict resolution skills, often the rule in marriages headed for divorce, affect a child's own ability to handle personal conflict.[8]

I believe that divorce should be labeled "Hazardous to a Child's Health." When God's plan for marriage and for the raising of children is disrupted, the consequences to the child can be devastating.

The Stepfamily: Not a Perfect Alternative

It has been said that in a few years the stepfamily will be the typical family structure in our culture. While many people—through patience, hard work, and devotion—successfully make the adjustments needed to live successfully as a stepfamily, "blended families" often face serious difficulties.

First of all, the role of stepparent is not always a pleasant one. The average stepfamily requires about six years to gel. This can be a difficult adjustment for children, who can feel as if they're living in two "countries," each with their own rules and customs. They hold citizenship in each and therefore are invested in the quality of life found in both. Some parents make the situation worse by trampling on their child's loyalties in an effort to get them to remain loyal to them. Some children feel they're part of a POW swap every other weekend.[9]

Is it any wonder that remarriages and stepfamilies can actually produce more problems simply because, as I pointed out earlier, they often produce additional divorces? An article in *Psychology Today* underscored this point: "Stepfamilies are such a minefield of divided loyalties, emotional traps and management conflicts that they are the most fragile form of family in America, breaking up at a rate even greater than that of first marriages."[10]

What's worse is that remarriage doesn't counteract the negative effects of divorce for children. On the contrary, there are indications that some children might be better off in a single-parent family than living in a stepfamily. I've seen this time and time again in both premarital and marital counseling with stepfamilies.

Now that we've looked at the problem of divorce, let's discuss some of the solutions. This is where our role as Marriage Keepers comes into play.

Being Part of the Solution

When someone is thinking of divorce, the first thing that person does is find others who will agree with and support the direction they're taking. They do that because they want to reinforce the way they're thinking and feeling.

We need couples who believe in marriage and who have healthy marriages themselves to come alongside those who are considering divorce and *not* agree with the direction they're taking, but instead provide a hope-filled, positive alternative: namely, working on their marriages.

Let's return to your friend from at the beginning of this chapter. Here is one way you might respond to her when she tells you she's getting a divorce: "It's true that divorce is one option, and since you're considering this path, let's go on a field trip and attend a divorce recovery workshop together so we can hear the stories of some people who are going through divorce right now."

Most people who haven't had to endure a divorce have no idea the kind of pain involved in divorce or the amount of adjustment it takes to weather it. Oftentimes, listening to the stories of people who are presently going through a divorce is a good reality check for those considering it. It can even send the man or woman in the direction of staying in and saving the marriage.

The grief involved in a divorce can be as intense as—or worse than—losing a loved one to death. The difference is that in a divorce with children, there is no closure—the connection between the two people who divorced remains. As one husband said to me, "Norm, I have my children every other weekend. But on those Sunday evenings when I take them home, I grieve all over again. It's been over ten years. Won't the loss and grief ever go away?"

Most people don't have the training it takes to counsel those who are on the brink of divorce. But that doesn't mean they can't help out when they see a marital breakup on the horizon. On the contrary, anyone can suggest some divorce alternatives, many of which are in operation right now.

Suggesting Some Alternatives to Divorce

The first place a couple who is on the brink of divorce should be sent is to their local church. The local church can often help out directly by providing counseling, and some are willing to pay for up to ten sessions of professional marriage counseling.

However, there are many other sources for "faith-based" marriage counseling services all over the nation. Here are some examples:

- *The Smalley Marriage Institute* in Branson, Missouri, provides intensive marriage counseling. At the time of this writing some 250 couples have participated in this intensive counseling program. Seventy percent of these participants were on the brink of divorce, but preliminary research suggests that 93 percent of couples have stayed together and have indicated that their marital satisfaction has improved.

- *The Association of Marriage and Family Ministries* (AMFM), a recently formed organization, trains and equips ministers, laypersons, and marriage and family educators to work directly within the church to build strong, Christ-centered marriage and families. Its primary focus is to train those in the local church to develop an ongoing ministry for married couples and families. (The website address is provided at the conclusion of this chapter.)

- *Smart Marriages* is an organization bringing together two thousand researchers, psychologists, therapists, pastors, church workers, chaplains, and government officials for the purpose of strengthening marriages in all areas of the country. (It's encouraging to see that it's not just the Christian community that cares about marriage.)

This is just the beginning of efforts nationwide to save and strengthen marriages. For example, many churches are working to become Marriage Keepers by strengthening marriage preparation.

Saving Marriages Before They Start

For too long, our culture has seen the church's role in marriage as just providing a place for the wedding. But God calls His church not just to perform weddings but to nurture marriages.

Many communities have now established a Community Marriage Policy in which churches agree to require premarital preparation for every couple seeking marriage. No counseling, no wedding, no exceptions. This policy also includes a strong ongoing mentoring program for several years following the wedding. The marriage policy is having an impact on the divorce rates in many of the places where it has been tried.

The following is an example of a church's promoting a covenant agreement in marriage: One church has each couple who wants to marry stand before the congregation. Those in attendance are asked to uphold the couple in prayer and to be available for counsel. The couple is asked to sign a covenant agreement to remain in a premarital preparation course from that moment until their wedding, whether it be for two months or a year. They also agree to abstain from sexual relations until the wedding night.

Here is another, more formal format:

The following process is designed to facilitate this preparation for couples getting married at Community Presbyterian Church. These are minimal requirements.

We agree to meet with the minister for an introduction to the marriage-preparation process.

We agree to complete six to eight sessions with a Christian professional therapist, including the following components: family history assessment, relationship profile (PREPARE), personality profile, and follow-up counseling session(s) during the first year of marriage.

We agree to meet with a mentor couple and work through a practical workbook for marriage preparation.

We agree to attend a four-hour seminar on Building Marriage God's Way.

If recommended by the pastor or counselor, we agree to participate in special programs for healing the past (in cases of divorce, addiction, etc.).

We agree to honor God by abstaining from sexual activity until marriage.

Today's date: _____

Prospective groom (print): _____
Signature: _____

Prospective bride (print): _____
Signature: _____

"What God has joined together, let man not separate." —Matthew 19:6

These churches are serious about preserving and strengthening marriage in their communities through premarital counseling. Thirty years ago, churches lacked the kinds of materials for marriage preparation that we have today for either the premarital preparation or the mentoring process.

Premarital counseling is one of the best forms of divorce prevention available. I know of example after example of churches that have cut their divorce rates by simply preparing people for married life *before* the wedding.

Now, let's take a look at the value of support *after* the wedding.

Some Postnuptial Support

We in the body of Christ need to take the support of marriages to a new level. Traditionally, we are there to support the couple during the wedding, but afterward we quickly forget to support the newlywed couple through prayer and counseling.

I've often wondered what would happen if we ministered to married couples at the beginning of their married life the way we minister to a bereaved family member when they lose a loved one. Many people put the name of the bereaved family on their calendar so they can remind themselves to contact the family member with a letter of support.

I believe that something like that could be done for newlyweds. Those who chose to participate in a program like that through their local church would be asked to sign up to write one letter of marital encouragement on one month during the couple's first five years of marriage and send it to them. This would be another expression of being a Marriage Keeper.

Every marriage needs the support of a community of believers. When a couple marries, the community rejoices; but when a couple divorces, the community grieves. For that reason, the community needs to make it a point to continue supporting the newly married couple after the wedding.

William Doherty suggests a model for this type of support:

> If we agree to be stakeholders in one another's marriages, sometimes the support we offer or receive is not going to be of the "feel good" variety. Sometimes it will come in the form of stubborn refusal to give up on someone's marriage. One group of twelve couples who socialized together for many years and grew to know one another's marriages without a lot of explicit talk about their relationships, faced the prospect of the divorce of one of the couples. The other couples rallied, talked extensively with both spouses, got them to a good therapist, and nurtured them through their crisis to a better relationship beyond. Weren't they being intrusive? You bet. The phrase they used was, "We don't want to lose one of our own." Just as they had done for couples who faced physical illness, this group rallied around a couple facing a marital illness. Instead of stepping back and just saying, "It's a private matter" or "It's their choice," they held the couple up until they healed. They helped their friends and community members cling as a couple until the new glue could congeal.[11]

Churches from coast to coast are moving more and more toward being Marriage Keepers as part of their ministries. A number of them are implementing "Reconciling God's Way," a program for struggling couples who have either filed for divorce or are considering it. It is a very structured program with thirteen-week classes, support groups, and a print and video curriculum. And perhaps most important, the leaders and facilitators teach from experience: They are all couples who have restored their troubled marriages.

I talked with leaders from several churches that had such programs and left each conversation very encouraged by the reports I heard about the results. One example of this is Killearn United Methodist Church in Tallahassee, Florida, which operates such a program and has seen just two divorces among the fifty to sixty couples who have completed the course.

This ministry—along with a Premarital Community Marriage Policy in effect—has also been very active, strong, and productive in the Modesto, California, area. As a result, over the past fifteen years the divorce rate in this community has dropped significantly.

Also, Canyon Hills Community Church in Bothell, Washington, has graduated scores of troubled couples from its program and has also established the ministry in several churches in the area. When these class sessions begin, many of the couples in attendance are barely talking to one another, but by the third or fourth session things begin to thaw between them. Finally, on graduation night, couples give their testimonies of how God healed their marriage; some even bring their divorce papers and tear them up in front of the class.

As you can see, there are a number of church-related ministries for the preservation or saving of marriages. But what can we as individuals do when we find out that someone we know is thinking of divorcing? Here are some ideas.

Before Speaking, Listen—but Speak!

When someone tells you he or she is about to divorce, it is your responsibility as a believer and as a Marriage Keeper to say something in support of marriage and of staying together. But it is important that you take the time to listen before you speak.

When your friend or family member tells you he or she is divorcing, you can start by saying something like, "Let's get together. I'd like to hear your story." When you meet with that person, just listen…and then listen some more. The Bible has some good things to say about listening before you speak, including the following: "He who answers before listening— that is his folly and his shame" (Proverbs 18:13).

As you listen, be prepared to hear things you don't want to hear and things you don't agree with. Also, remember that the person you are listening to believes in his or her heart that they are the innocent party in the situation. Be prepared to hear everything that person sees as wrong in the marriage and with the spouse.

Eventually, after you've listened to what the person has to say, you're going to have to offer what you have to say about their plans to divorce. There are some simple questions or statements you can use to help turn their thinking away from divorce. Here is a good place to start:

"You've told me what's wrong with your marriage and what isn't working. Now tell me what's *right* about it and what *is* working." If you hear, "Nothing!" the first time you ask, then repeat your question until you help the person turn his or her thinking in a new direction.

As I've counseled married couples over the past decade, I've found that the majority of marriages had more positives and strengths going for them than negatives or weaknesses. However, we humans have a tendency to fix a radar lock on what isn't working or what's lacking in our situations. When we focus on the problems and negatives, the positives tend to fall by the wayside.

For that reason, questions that move a person in a different direction in their thinking can generate hope. For example, you can ask, "What was one pleasant time you experienced with your spouse this week?" After the answer, ask the person for another example of a pleasant time.

Then get down to talking about the spouse, asking questions such as, "What do you appreciate about your spouse?" and "What are three of his [or her] positive qualities?"

Here is an example of a statement you could make to intervene in the life of someone contemplating divorce:

"You're thinking that you don't love your spouse and that you can't fall in love again. But think about this for a minute: When you first got married, how would you have responded if someone had suggested that in X number of years, you would fall out of love? You'd have told them they were crazy! You wouldn't have believed them, would you? The positive feelings you had for your spouse at that time would have kept you from even considering such an idea, right? Well, it works the other way as well. Your *negative* feelings are getting in the way of giving thought to the idea of rekindling your love for your spouse. But it is still possible!"

Here is another example:

"I appreciate your willingness to let me know what you're experiencing. Let me ask just one question: If there was any chance at all for restoration—even if it required a miracle—would you take that chance? If your marriage could be turned around and the love you once had for your spouse could be restored—if you could begin to find what you wanted in marriage in the first place *and* avoid the financial and emotional devastation of divorce for you and your children—would you give it a shot?"

Someone would have to be deeply hurt and hardened not to at least consider that idea. In that case, it would be wise to suggest that the person take a "cooling off" period before proceeding with a divorce. It would also be wise to suggest intensive professional counseling and perhaps read and invest in some materials designed to help people restore their marriages. (See Recommended Reading and Resources at the end of this chapter.)

How often does a despairing couple who is ready for

divorce hear words like these? Sometimes these words will fall on deaf ears, but at other times the couple who hears them will listen and try what you've suggested.

Either way, we should never stop being advocates for marriage. We should be willing to speak up, even if what we say makes others uncomfortable. God's plan and purpose is for marriage to not only last but also bring honor and glory to Him. Marriages are worth saving. And it may be up to you!

For Your Consideration

1. What are you doing to safeguard your marriage?
2. If your own parents divorced, how has this impacted you and what will you do to counter the effects?
3. What is your church doing to actively encourage marriage and discourage divorce?
4. What will you say to the next person you hear is considering divorce?

Recommended Reading and Resources

AUDIOVISUAL RESOURCES

Love Life, Dr. Ed Wheat (audio).

Choosing Wisely, Before You Divorce (video).

Divorce Care for Kids. A twelve-session, video-based group divorce recovery program for children.

Note: All three of these audiovisual resources can be obtained through Christian Marriage Enrichment,

PO Box 2468, Orange, CA 92859; or call (800) 875-7560.

B O O K S

Take Back Your Marriage by William Doherty (Guilford, 2001).

When the Vow Breaks: A Survival and Recovery Guide for Christians Facing Divorce by Joseph Warren Kiniskern (Broadman & Holman, 1993). This is one of the best resources available. Includes a section on what the Bible says about divorce.

R E S O U R C E S   F O R   S A V I N G   M A R R I A G E S

The Smalley Marriage Institute, (866) 875-2915, www.smalleymarriage.com.

Reconciling God's Way, PO Box 1543, Modesto, CA 95353, (800) 205-6808, www.valleymarriageresources.org.

P R E M A R I T A L   P R E P A R A T I O N   R E S O U R C E S

The Premarital Counseling Handbook, H. Norman Wright (Moody Press, 1992).

Mentoring Engaged and Newlywed Couples Participant's Guide by Drs. Les & Leslie Parrott (Zondervan, 1997).

Association of Marriage and Family Ministries (AMFM) website: www.amfmonline.com.

Chapter Eight

THE BENEFITS
OF MARRIAGE:
A CAREFULLY
GUARDED SECRET

IMAGINE YOURSELF standing in front of a room filled with a hundred men and women. They're sharp, educated, risers in their professions, unmarried, and most in their twenties and early thirties. Some are considering marriage, others are neutral, and a few are dead set against it. You've been invited to come and lead a discussion titled "Why Marriage?" This group is like any you'd find in a university class or church singles group, meaning that some of the young people will be receptive to the idea of marriage, while others will be antagonistic.

You may be thinking, *Norm, that's something you may be able to do, but not me. You're the teacher, the speaker, the so-called expert on marriage. You can talk to them on this subject, but I cannot.*

But what if a young couple approached you and your spouse and asked you, "Why do you believe in marriage? Why should anyone marry? What are we going to get out of it?" Good questions indeed. But it's not good enough to answer the question "Why do you believe in marriage?" by saying, "Because we're married." Each of us needs to be able to tell others why we value marriage and why we're married ourselves. That's part of being Marriage Keepers.

What's So Great About Marriage?

If I had to speak to the group of a hundred young people I mentioned above, I'd begin with the same question I've asked thousands to answer over the years as I've taught in college and young adult settings: "What will you get out of marriage that you wouldn't get if you remained single?"

"What's it going to do for *me*?" Isn't that the question most ask when it comes to marriage? The truth is, most people aren't going to marry unless they're convinced they're going to benefit from it. Many will say of getting married, "I want to meet the needs of my spouse" or "I want to help him/her feel loved." That may be true for a lot of people, but without the assurance that we're getting something out of being married, the vast majority of us wouldn't do it.

As I've sat with engaged couples in my counseling office over the years and asked them, "What are twelve reasons you want to marry your partner?" I could hear what they were saying, even when they didn't verbalize it. Between the lines of their answers was this message: "This is what I hope to get out of being married." Some found what they were looking for in marriage, while others didn't.

Unfortunately, most of us don't enter into marriage with a servant's heart. A few do, but for the others it's a matter of hoping that it develops over time.

There are exceptions to this rule, however. Some couples actually do marry with a commitment to be a servant. Such was the case with Dave and Lisa. For them, being servants to one another was the only way it could work.

You see, there were issues for Dave and Lisa to overcome. First of all, there was a major age difference, and second, there were children from a previous marriage. But the biggest issue this couple faced was Dave's multiple sclerosis.

Ten years before Dave and Lisa were married, Dave was diagnosed with MS and given five years to live. However, Dave's body didn't heed the doctor's prognosis. Lisa was twenty-four on their wedding day, and Dave was forty-one. Lisa married Dave with the full knowledge that she would be a young widow in just a few years. But Lisa's commitment to Dave was to be his wife, not his caretaker or nurse. She pledged to be his hands and feet when he needed them, but most of all she pledged to be his wife.

It's hard to imagine the adjustments this couple had to make in order to make their marriage work. Dave was no longer able to work, so they were faced with the question of who would provide financially. Then there was the age difference—almost a generation between them. Added to that was the challenge of having a sexual relationship, as well as caring for the children.

Somehow, because of God's help, Lisa's determination, and Dave's optimistic view of life, they overcame all odds and obstacles and made the adjustments necessary to have a happy marriage.

David and Lisa's wedding took two hours and was one of the most fulfilling and emotional weddings I've ever taken part in. In the program, there was a page for each wedding participant to fill out that said the following:

Dear Family and Friends,

As we stated in our invitation: "Because you are the people who have touched our lives, we are asking you to participate with us and to make a commitment to be more than witnesses."

So would you please take some time to share with us some words of wisdom, a prayer, or an experience in your life that could help us grow and give us guidance as we embark upon life together?

We will be keeping all your thoughts in a notebook prepared for us, close at hand and close to our hearts, because "where there is no guidance the people fall, but in abundance of counselors there is victory" (Proverbs 11:14, NASB).

Your name: _____

After the ceremony, as we made our way out of the sanctuary into the foyer, I noticed scores of completed forms on the table. When we met with Dave and Lisa six months later for their marital checkup, they showed us a scrapbook filled with stories and words of wisdom from more than a hundred marriages.

Many couples assisted Dave and Lisa in various ways in their marriage, which happened against all odds but which was a good and fulfilling relationship for them both. They endured inconvenience and obstacles most people can't even imagine, but with God at the center of their marriage, they made it work. The ten years they had together was well worth the sacrifices for both of them.

Eventually, Dave was confined to a wheelchair and then to bed. One day Lisa called and told me, "We've hired a caretaker to care for Dave. I don't want to be that for him. I want to remain his wife and lover." And that she was, every moment of their marriage.

A few weeks later Dave died, and at his memorial service there was more laughter than tears. I know I miss Dave. I miss his love for Jesus and the songs he wrote, played, and sang. I miss his laughter. So does Lisa and their two daughters. But this was a marriage that taught others some important lessons. It will be remembered as a marriage that was a success because both the man and the woman had servant's hearts.

David and Lisa had the kind of marriage that the group of one hundred single people I talked about at the beginning of this chapter need to see. And it's the kind of marriage we're all called to have. It's a marriage that answers the question, "Why should we get married?"

Marriage: Still in God's Script

Isn't it interesting that marriage, which has always been accepted as "the norm" in our culture, has been thrust into the center of a storm of controversy? Marriage has shifted in our culture's thinking from something that used to be necessary or almost mandatory to optional—and a high-risk option at that.

It's not that people don't want to marry. Many do, but on two conditions—that it's happy and that it lasts. Christians still marry; in fact, they marry in higher percentages than nonbelievers. But they have concerns. They see marriage as being under attack. Who ever would have thought we'd be on the verge of living in a post-marriage culture?[1]

When marriage as an institution comes under attack, there's a ripple effect throughout society. In our culture, the alternative of living together is the new norm, and the presence of both parents in the home of a child isn't considered vital. Seeing two same-gender parents is no longer an oddity. The word *marriage* is even disappearing from many books and magazines, replaced by the word *couple*.

Even we as Christians have fallen into this cultural trap. When we hear about these new family configurations, instead of saying, "That's not the way God intended it to be, so let's look at the biblical model," we remain silent, implying either acceptance or approval.

Marriage is and always will be a good, strong, positive word that reflects God's plan for couples and for families. He is the Creator of the script. And as Marriage Keepers, we are to keep that script for ourselves and others.

Advantages to Being Married?

Now let's return to the gathering of the hundred single men and women from the beginning of the chapter. It is safe to assume that many of them 1) have a negative attitude toward marriage, 2) are soured on the idea of marriage because of their parents' or friends' negative experiences, 3) will be resistant to whatever you have to say about marriage, and/or 4) couldn't care less about the facts of marriage.

These four attitudes are becoming more and more prevalent among single men and women in our society. If I had to speak to this group, I would start by telling them about some of the practical advantages to marriage, starting with those relating to longevity and health.

I would begin the longevity and health questions by asking the people how long they would like to live. When I threw out the ages of fifty and sixty, everyone there raised their hands. Starting with the age of seventy, the number of raised hands started decreasing, because the young people began considering quality of life rather than duration.

As I asked these questions, I would find that everybody agreed that they wanted to live a good, long, and healthy life. "So," I'd say, "all of you want to live to be somewhere in your nineties, in good health, able to make love, and die in your sleep. Right?" The laughter and smiles in the room would speak volumes. But when I'd ask these people what they were doing to stay healthy, here are some of the answers I would hear:

- "I practice yoga."
- "I don't eat red meat."
- "I run five miles a day."
- "I have an active sex life."
- "I use a personal trainer to keep me in shape."
- "I eat vegetables—solid vegetables three times a day."
- "I have two dogs and a cat. Who needs anything else?"
- "I take vitamins and eat health foods, especially carrot juice."
- "I eliminate stress. That's why I don't date."

This would be a very health-conscious group who planned to live long lives and stay in good health. Knowing that, I begin to spring my facts on them about long lives, good health, and marriage.

"Now, you may be surprised at what I have to say next," I would say, "But most of you in this room will end up married, and if you want to live long and stay healthy you will really *want* to be married. Why? Because you're a very health-conscious group who wants to live a long time, and the most important ingredient for a long, healthy life is marriage."

Indeed, marriage is a lifesaver—or at least a life prolonger. Young, healthy people don't usually think much about health risks associated with their lifestyles, but statistics show that those who remain unmarried have higher incidences—leading to higher death rates—of the following:

- Coronary and heart disease, or in plain language, heart attacks and heart failure. One study showed that a married man who has heart disease can be expected to live, on average, fourteen hundred days longer than an unmarried man with a healthy heart.[2]

- Stroke.
- Pneumonia.
- Cancer—many varieties.
- Cirrhosis of the liver.
- Automobile accidents.
- Murder.
- Suicide.

The biblical phrase "It is not good for man to be alone" takes on a new ring when you read the above, doesn't it? But it's also true of women who remained unmarried. That is true in the United States and in other nations and cultures.[3]

Marriage really does contribute to a longer, healthier life, and married people seem to know it. When married men and women are asked how they would rate their own health, they tend to say that they feel healthier than those who are divorced, separated, or widowed.[4]

"Some of you are probably very proactive," I would challenge my group of one hundred. "You're movers and shakers in your business. But some of you are afraid of and avoiding something: marriage. And why are you doing that? We only have one life to live here on earth, and I would think you'd want to be here as long as you can and get the most out of it while you're here."

The statistics would back me up on that, too. Studies have shown that almost nine out of ten married men who are alive at age forty-eight are still alive at sixty-five. On the other hand, among men who never marry, only six out of ten alive at age forty-eight would make it to sixty-five.[5] Marriage tends to enhance women's lifespans also, although not as dramatically as it does for men.[6]

A Longer Life for Marrieds? How Could That Be?

My next question for my hundred guests would be this: "What is it about marriage that makes a difference? Why do married people—especially the men—tend to live longer and remain healthier than single people?"

It's fairly simple, really. Marriage tends to settle men down and change some of their not-too-smart behaviors. Single men tend to abuse alcohol, drive intoxicated, or smoke (all unhealthy, potentially self-destructive behaviors) more than married men. Also, married men are only half as likely as singles to take their own lives.

Now it's time for me to step on some toes, time for me to get a little controversial. "Men live longer because of their wives," I tell the young people. And why? "While no man particularly likes being controlled (no one does), wives very often monitor and influence some of their husband's habits and behaviors. They monitor how their husbands eat, drive, smoke, and rest. And while men tend to put off doctor and dental visits, their wives often make sure the medical and dental checkups—as well as other doctor and dentist visits—are happening. Of course, this is very beneficial for a man."

We men are notorious for procrastinating when it comes to seeing a doctor, even when symptoms yell, "You're in trouble!" Sometimes that's because we don't want our fears about our health confirmed. A close friend of mine is an example of that. For three days, he suffered with chest and arm pains before he finally went to the doctor—at the strong urging of his wife. His checkup revealed that he had two arteries 100 percent blocked and a third 90 percent blocked. When the doctor asked my friend why he hadn't come in earlier, his response was, "Hey, I'm a guy. You know we put this stuff off." After a five-way bypass operation, he has become very compliant as his wife monitors his daily walking and diet.

The Emotional Benefits of Marriage

The next thing I would tell my single friends is that we men need our wives to oversee our health—not just our physical health, but our emotional health as well. It has been shown that the empathy and concern of a marriage partner helps in reducing both stress and depression.[7]

"The level of commitment marriage brings can contribute to a deeper sense of meaning in life," I tell them. "When you feel a sense of responsibility for a spouse and children, you realize that you're truly in a family unit and that others are depending upon you."

Mental health is a major concern in our society—everyone wants to avoid depression and anxiety. And who do you think is less likely to feel depressed or anxious or to have other physiological distress? Those who are married! Married people are generally much happier and less stressed than those who are single, widowed, or divorced. That statistic applies to both men and women.

About this time in our discussion, someone in the crowd will challenge me: "It's not marriage itself that makes people happier, more satisfied, and healthier. It's the other way around—happy, satisfied, healthy people find it easier to get and keep a spouse."

Now I have to tell the young people in the room that the research just doesn't validate that assertion. It's not the people going into marriage that make the difference when it comes to health and happiness—it's the dynamic of marriage itself. Marriage provides us someone to be there for us. We don't face life alone.

So the bottom line is this: If you want your mental health to improve, marry.[8]

SEX! Now That I Have Your Attention

I know my audience has been waiting for this one! I tell them that traditionally, one of the reasons for marriage has been sex. Originally, marriage was *the* place to have sex, but today it's not limited to marriage, nor does it seem to be a major reason for getting married.

Sex is not a subject people speak about in hushed tones anymore. It is now used to sell everything imaginable, the implication being that if you use a certain product you'll have more and better sex. Even in the Christian marketplace, books and study guides about sex abound, including titles such as

Intended for Pleasure, The Celebration of Sex, Sheet Music, Men and Sex, and *The Gift of Sex.*

Who needs marriage for sex? You do! I'm not talking about that just from a Christian, biblical standpoint, both of which are very clear about the purpose and place of sex. It's just that there are numerous reasons why marriage is the best arrangement for a sexual relationship.

First of all, there is the proximity factor in a marriage. In other words, when all is said and done, it's easier for those who are married to have sex. It fits their lifestyle simply because they're not out searching for a partner or taking the risks.

Having a permanent relationship with one person gives us the freedom and incentive we need to invest time and energy into creating a fulfilling sex life. Our goal in that case should be to discover our partner's needs and desires and meet those. Naturally, there are benefits for each of us in doing just that. We also need to keep the safety factor in mind. With multiple partners who also have multiple partners, there is more risk of disease.

A marital sexual relationship contributes to emotional bonding that enhances the satisfaction level. And when we add the ongoing development of spiritual intimacy with a spouse, sexual satisfaction with this special person can soar.

So our bottom line on this subject is that the best sex is in marriage.[9]

It's Also a Matter of Economics

I don't know many people—men or women—who don't want to be financially successful. Well, the numbers tell us that being married increases one's chances of being just that. I would make sure the group I was talking to knew the facts about this.

I've heard many single people say that they're the exception, that they're better off being single because they don't have to care for anyone else and therefore have more money to spend on themselves. Depending on the individual, that may or may not be true. However, it's hard to argue with the facts.

I've met some who are offended by discussing marriage as an economic benefit. To them, that seems to reduce marriage to a financial arrangement between families, much as countries in the past have formed alliances between themselves in order to protect themselves against war.

Of course, most people don't get married because of the monetary gains many people enjoy in marriage. On the other hand, I don't think most realize the financial differences between marrieds and unmarrieds. And the statistics tell us that both men *and* women who take the step of marriage generally end up with higher average household incomes than those who are single.

Why do you think this is? Generally speaking, being married increases a man's sense of responsibility and of productivity, which leads to a higher income. Men tend to specialize in how they earn money, and it has been shown that with the support of a wife in other areas of their lives, men are free to focus more on their work and on earning money. Furthermore, the "settling" effects of marriage tend to make men better workers. As a rule, the longer a man is married, the greater his earning power. The following quote summarizes this well: "The close working relationship between a man and woman in marriage seems key to increasing man's earnings."[10]

As I presented this information to the group of one hundred, I could sense very strongly that the young women, who made up roughly half the group, would want to hear what's in it for them.

Well, what about a married woman who works? She also tends to earn more and is also able to share in her husband's financial success. Apparently, the "ours" of marriage does better financially than the "mine" of remaining single or living together.

We've already seen that those who marry tend to earn more. It only follows that being married encourages the creation and retention of wealth.[11] In other words, the longer a couple stays married, the more they accumulate financially. Naturally, this benefits the children in the marriage also.[12] The converse is true also—the longer someone who has been divorced stays unmarried, the less they tend to have.

The pooling of resources and material goods in a marriage contributes to the wealth of the couple. They share many of the same items, and their joint savings, retirement plans, and medical coverage benefit both.

For those in the crowd who are into facts and figures, the following may resonate: "Two economists calculated how much spouses gain from pooling their risks in marriages. Just getting married creates an annuity value that is equal to increasing one's wealth by 12 to 14 percent at the age of thirty and by 30 percent at the age of seventy-five, compared to staying single. We don't count these windfalls in wealth from marriage in any official statistics, so the astoundingly greater wealth of the married that we noted earlier is really even bigger than it looks."[13]

Another factor in the generally higher levels of income and living standards of married people is the added sense of accountability and responsibility marriage tends to give both people.

Here's what I'm talking about.

When you are married, can you just plunge ahead on a major purchase? When you get the impulse to buy a boat, a new car, or a plasma TV, do you just buy it without consulting your spouse? Well, if you did, you'd be headed for trouble! Those who are married need to think about their spouse; they can't just "live for themselves" the way they did when they were single. When you're married you tend to act more cautiously and responsibly with what you have.

In Summary...

After I presented all this information to this group of young singles, I'd have to ask them if these are reasons sufficient to encourage them to marry. Well, in and of themselves, none of them is a good reason to get married. These are just some of the added benefits of marriage. From the standpoint of health, sex, wealth, and general happiness, marriage makes sense.

The information in this chapter gives single people and married people alike some things to think about. If you're single, you can see that marriage is a positive choice for a lot of reasons. If you're married, it can help you see your relationship with your spouse from a different perspective.

For you married people, when is the last time you and your spouse identified the benefits of being married? Have you thanked God recently for your marriage? Have you thanked your spouse for who he or she is and for what your spouse has contributed to your marriage? Have you discussed together what you have because of being married?

More important, who will you share this information with? As Marriage Keepers, we are called not to hoard this information. We should share it with children, neighbors, small groups, or Sunday school class members—even with those who may have negative attitudes toward marriage.

As we do all these things, we need to keep in mind that marriage is God's idea, not man's. It's His plan for the family and for us as couples, and it's a better plan than anyone else has offered. God knew what He was doing when He said, "It's not good for man to be alone." It was the beginning of His script.

For Your Consideration

1. What are some good reasons for getting married?
2. What are you getting out of marriage that you wouldn't have gotten if you'd remained single?
3. Ask yourself, *What is it like being married to me?*

Chapter Nine

YOUR
MARRIAGE
STORY

WHEN MY DAUGHTER Sheryl was young, some of my favorite moments with her were when she would say, "Daddy, tell me about you when you were a little boy." Off I would go, recounting stories long ago put on the shelf.

Life is full of stories…life *is* a story. The tales we tell paint pictures in our minds and remind us of our own experiences, evoking an array of emotions. This can inspire us, challenge us, motivate us, and take us out of our world and into another, if only for a few brief moments. Whether or not we're aware we're doing it, we all tell stories in one way or another. Some of our stories we're eager to tell; others we wish we could just hide forever.

For years many people have listened to stories by Garrison Keillor as he weaves tales about life in the fictional Lake Wobegon. The way he uses descriptions and details, you feel as though you're there—seeing the images, hearing the sounds, smelling the fragrances (some were odors), and smiling and laughing. As his stories draw to a close, you don't want the experience to end.

Joyce and I would often listen to Keillor on *A Prairie Home Companion* as we drove home. When we arrived, we didn't want to leave the car before the story was over, so we'd often sit and listen. When the story concluded, we would sit silently together, enjoying what we had heard.

As I write this, I realize these times have become special memories that make up our own marital story that has come from being together for over forty-five years.

As we move through life, we accumulate experiences that can be crafted into stories. One of the stories we should want to add to year after year—and tell to as many who will listen—is the one about our marriage. Unfortunately, some married people don't have much of a story to tell. Theirs was disrupted by a permanent detour. However, telling your story regularly can be a safeguard against disruption.

As one author advised:

Tell your [marital] story. Tell it to your kids, your friends, your brothers and sisters, but especially to each other. The more your story is implanted in your brain, the more it serves as a hedge against the myriad forces that seek to destroy your marriage. Make your story so familiar that it becomes part of the fabric of your being. It should be a legend that is shared through the generations as you grow a family tree that defies all odds and boasts marriage after marriage of stability, strength, and longevity.[1]

What do you know about the marriages in your family tree? Do any come to mind? What is the legend of your parents' marriage?

Different Couples, Different Stories

As a marriage counselor, I've heard many marriage stories over the years. Sadly, many of the stories I've heard were of disrupted marriages. All the husband and wife wanted to talk about were the problems in their marriage.

However, I found that when I asked these couples to share the "other side" of their marriages—the one they overlooked— I began to hear a good story. I would ask them how and where they met and what attracted them to one another, what their first date was like, how the first year of marriage went, what each of them did well, what they appreciated about one another, and what they saw as the strengths in their relationship. Before long, not only did these couples end up with a good and balanced story, but they realized they had much to be thankful for. They would also realize that they had been overlooking the good side of their marriage because they had failed to follow one part of the script from Paul: "Think about the things that are true and honorable and right and pure and beautiful and respected" (Philippians 4:8, NCV).

The other side of my career as a marriage counselor is that I've heard many great examples of marriage stories, the kind all of us—married and unmarried alike—need to hear.

For more than thirty years I've conducted Marriage Enrichment seminars all over the country. For twelve years we held a weeklong seminar every fall at the Grand Teton National Park in Wyoming. We always had a mixture of ages at our seminars, and these were no exception. One day, as some of the older couples were sharing their stories—some of which contained ideas that other couples borrowed to improve their own marriages—I observed that the younger couples were hanging on their words, trying to learn things that would help them in their relationships.

I also read the story of a wife who reported that she and her husband had written a daily love letter to each other for the past twenty-five years of their marriage. They never missed a day, even when the husband had open-heart surgery, and they've saved between eighteen and nineteen thousand of these letters so that when they're gone their children can read them.[2]

Another couple I knew of enjoyed their wedding so much that they've had another wedding every year—for the past fifteen years! Each year, this couple has a wedding at a different location, with a different minister, in a different church, and with different traditions. Sometimes this couple's friends and family are there, sometimes not. But since they always have a photographer at their weddings, they now have more than fifteen photo albums filled with pictures from each year's wedding (in two of them, you can see that the wife is expecting). As this couple looks through their numerous photo albums, they reflect on the good times and the hardships from the previous years so that they can identify what they've learned and how they can improve their marriage in the coming years.

People like these, and others who take the time to tell their stories, are a treasure. I believe that if every church would encourage couples such as these to tell their marital stories— including their successes and failures—it would be a tremendous blessing to those in their twenties and thirties, whether they were married or single.

That is Marriage Keeping!

Now ask yourself, *What are we doing to preserve our experiences and our story?* What would you say if you were to tell your story?

What's Your Story?

When you and your spouse tell the story of your marriage, it could be a blessing to a lot of people around you. But what about blessing one another with it?

Do you and your spouse ever take the time to tell your story to *one another*? Have you ever sat holding hands with your spouse and shared the story of your marriage? It can be quite an intimate experience, one where you will probably get choked up, cry, and laugh. You may even feel a bit of conviction, delight, satisfaction, or amazement.

Some couples make sharing their marriage stories an annual practice, and they usually do it on their anniversary.

In our marriage seminars, we ask couples to reflect back on their courtship, engagement, and early part of their marriage by having them finish the following sentences:

- "On our first date we…"
- "When we were dating, we had the most fun when…"
- "Our favorite song was…"
- "I was attracted to my mate because…"
- "My spouse was attracted to me because…"
- "What I remember most about our wedding was…"
- "At the proposal, the question was…"
- "On our honeymoon, we…"

We also have the couple share their finished sentences—as well as some of their wedding pictures—with several other couples. It's a time of remembering experiences and feelings, some perhaps long forgotten and in need of revival.

What responses do these questions evoke in you and your spouse right now? We so quickly forget what drew us to one another, but remembering your foundation just might help you continue persevering and growing. It also might help you add to your marital story.

It is inevitable that your marital story will change, simply because the marriage itself changes. You can't stop changes, but you can help direct some of them. Just as it took a great amount of time to complete some of the great statues or monuments of history, it takes time for your marriage to mature. Like your walk with Christ, your marriage is a "work in progress." For that reason, we need to stop now and again and ask ourselves two questions: "How is my Christian walk the same or different now than it was a year ago or five years ago?" and "How is my marriage the same or different now than it was a year ago or five years ago?"

Writing Your Story During Times of Change

As changes occur in your lives, it is your challenge as a married couple to use them to draw yourselves closer together rather than allow them to tear you apart. Throughout your married life you will suffer losses—some small, some large, some even devastating. You may have to endure miscarriages, stillbirths, job or career losses, illnesses, accidents, and any other of literally hundreds of setbacks. How you respond to each will affect your marriage relationship and the story your marriage tells.

When grief enters your lives, it can disrupt your life or throw it off course. Men and women tend to grieve differently, which can create a distance between two married people. When that happens, it's as though one is responding on AM and the other on FM. However, experiences with grief can cause a couple to grow closer than ever before. Any change carries with it the potential for growth if you face the changes head-on, tend to them, and then refine your relationship to bring it back into balance.

Perhaps the best way to handle the changes that occur in your marriage is to realize that you *will* go through change, loss, and crisis at some point in your life. Life is a journey that has a beginning and some type of conclusion. Its events follow a sequence and progression—sometimes smooth and orderly, other times rough and bumpy. Within this journey are stages or periods that might be called seasons. As Ecclesiastes states, "To every thing there is a season" (3:1, KJV).

Making Changes in Your Story
Through Words and Actions

Some changes in life seem to happen on their own, but others we *make* happen. It's commonly believed that one spouse can't do much to bring about changes in his or her marriage or even in the other spouse. That, however, is a myth.

Every person is an agent of change. Your words alone can put your spouse in a good mood or a bad mood; they can put a damper on their day or light your spouse up. When you change the way you speak or respond to your spouse, you will probably see changes in your spouse's response to you.

Since we're talking about changes, let's get practical and personal.

One of the best ways to improve a relationship for the better is to do the unexpected. In marriage, we learn to respond in the same old ways to the same old things. But that makes for a stagnant marriage with a boring story. If what you're doing in your marriage doesn't produce the results or changes you're after, then it might be time to try something different.

I remember one time when my wife, Joyce, did the unexpected:

During the early years of our marriage, I was fairly sloppy when it came to hanging up my pajamas in the morning. I took care of most of my other clothes, but in the morning when I took off my pj's I gave them a fling toward a hook in the closet, where they were supposed to go, or just tossed them on the bed. Joyce reminded me about it on numerous occasions, and each time I'd give verbal assent. Somehow, though, the message never took hold.

One day I was seated on the couch reading the newspaper, and Joyce came over and sat down next to me. She just waited until I turned toward her, and when I did I noticed that my pajamas were neatly folded on her lap. She put her arm around me, looked me in the eye, and said, "Norm, I just know that a man of your organizational ability and attention to detail and results would get a great sense of satisfaction going to work each day knowing that your pajamas were hanging neatly on the hook in the closet, where they would eagerly await your return at night. Thank you for listening."

With that, Joyce walked out of the room, leaving me there with my mouth hanging open. I didn't realize it until a couple of months later, but from that day forward I began hanging up my pajamas every morning. Joyce had gotten my attention in a new way, and I had listened.

Here's another change-through-something-different story from a wife:

I had been frustrated for some time with the lack of communication between my husband and me. Part of the problem was that his work took him away all week, and he was home only on the weekends. But when he was home, his interest was in sex, not talking. I felt a lot of resentment.

He also complained about me being away at church on Sunday morning, but that was a must for me. I'm a believer, and at that time he wasn't. I finally went to a marriage counselor for some suggestions. He sent me home with a book filled with suggestions to spark romance, and also a series of cassettes on the role of sex in marriage by Dr. Ed Wheat. I read and listened, and it finally dawned on me that if I wasn't getting my husband to talk to me, I'd better approach the communication problem in a new way.

The next weekend was my husband's birthday, so I dropped the children off at my parents' house, and Saturday night I took him to a very romantic restaurant. He seemed to enjoy it. When we came out of the restaurant we were next door to a Marriott Hotel. I stopped Terry, looked him in the eye and said, "Let's not go home tonight. Let's go in, get a room, and go up and take a bubble bath together."

He stopped in his tracks and just looked at me. When the shock wore off, he stammered, "Well, we can't!"

I asked, "Why not?"

"Well…I didn't bring my toothbrush."

At that point, I smiled, reached in my purse, and took out his toothbrush and a room key. I handed them to him and said, "Let's go!" And we did. It was great.

That night we talked for six hours. The next morning I skipped church and stayed in bed with my husband. That's where I felt the Lord wanted me to be that day. That night turned our relationship around. I guess there's something to this idea of meeting your partner's needs. It sure changed Terry's response to me.

Another wife shared this story about trying something different:

My husband and I had been married for less than a year. Since we had married a little later than most couples, Ted already owned his own well-furnished home. In the master bedroom, we had a large two-shelf stand, and on the top was a massive stereo with speakers and all the other components. I found it a bit unsightly and suggested we put the speakers and components on the lower shelf so I could decorate the top shelf with plates, vases, or plants. Ted didn't go for the idea and had his logical reasons for why the stereo should stay where it was. We discussed it several times, but he didn't even want to give it a try.

One day I decided to take a chance and move everything to the lower shelf. I spent some time arranging the top shelf in a new way. I tested the stereo to make sure it sounded all right.

When Ted came home and finally went into the bedroom, he saw the change, as well as a note that said, "This isn't permanent, just one of my wild experiments. Tell me what you think about it and test the sound. If you think it's okay and would like to keep it this way, we can. But if not, I'll be glad to put it back the way it was. Thanks for your input."

When he came down, he looked at me, smiled, and said, "Well...I like it. Let's give it a try." That's all I was asking for, the opportunity to try it.

Perhaps these stories can motivate and help you as you attempt to make changes in your marriage and in your home by "trying something different."

When Your Story Includes Difficulties

We all want a marriage that is everything we want it to be—with no upsets, no disruptions, and no detours along the way. That's certainly true for my wife and me.

Well, life is full of interruptions—sometimes divine interruptions. The unexpected and sudden events in life can teach you something new about your marriage relationship, namely, that marriage is a life of shared pain. None of us relishes the thought of pain. But when we're married, some of the days aren't bright and sunny but dark, overcast, and dreary. On days like that, it's easy to wonder if the sun will ever shine again.

Perhaps you've already been there. You've been through a job loss, an illness, a personal betrayal, economic changes, a disabled family member, the death of a family member, or the loss of your home. All of these, and other events like them, are losses that necessitate grief. If you've not been there yet, someday you will. That's not pessimism, but realism.

Recently, during a one-month span in my ministry as a grief and trauma counselor, I sat with a couple who had lost their two-year-old to a drowning accident, another couple whose two-month-old had died of SIDS, another who had lost a thirteen-year-old to a heart attack, another who had lost their fifteen-year-old in a car wreck, another whose sixteen-year-old had committed suicide, and still another whose twelve-year-old had been run over by a tractor.

How do couples survive their world and their marriage being turned upside down like this? It's only through the grace of God. It's through being in His presence and knowing His assurance and His strength that people make it through personal tragedies like these.

Joyce and I have been there, so we know about these things.

God's Part in Our Story

As God was there for those in Oklahoma City, New York City, and all other ground zeros, He was there for us when we noticed how our son Matthew's development had been delayed and when he suffered his first seizure. He was there when the neurologist from UCLA told us Matthew's brain had not formed properly and that mentally he would probably never advance beyond two years old. He was there through the seizures, through the nights when Matt sat up in his bed all night giggling, through the illnesses, through the frustrations of caring for a ninety-pound infant who couldn't feed himself or be potty trained. He was there leading us to place him in a Christian facility that could minister to him and care for him better than we could. He was there the morning of March 15, 1990, when He called Matthew home after a surgery and two-week hospital stay. And He was there during the years of grieving we felt as we brought scores of couples into our lives and ministered to them through our experience with Matthew.

Through all this we discovered the sufficiency of God's Word. "Consider it all joy, my brethren, when you encounter various trials, knowing that the testing [or trying] of your faith produces endurance" (James 1:2–3, NASB). It's easy to read a passage like this and agree with it in theory. It is another thing, however, to put it into practice.

What does the word *consider* actually mean in this context? It literally refers to an internal attitude of the heart and mind that allows a life trial to affect us either adversely or beneficially. Knowing that, another way we could translate James 1:2 might be: "Make up your mind to regard adversity as something to welcome or be glad about."

When you are going through trials and difficulties, you have the power to decide what your attitude will be. You can approach it and say something like, "This is terrible. Why is this happening to me now? *Why me?*" But you can also choose an attitude that says, "It's not what I wanted in life, but it's here. Now, what can I learn from it and how can it be used for God's glory?"

The verb tense used in the word *consider* indicates a decisiveness of action. It's not an attitude of resignation, one that causes us to just give up in the face of our troubles knowing we can't do anything to change them anyway. The verb tense actually indicates that you will have to go against your natural inclination to see the trial as a negative force.

There will be some moments in life and in your marriage when you won't see your trials that way, moments when you'll have to remind yourself that God wants to help you see your difficulties from a different perspective. When you do that, your mind will shift from resignation to a more constructive response.

Joyce and I did not anticipate becoming the parents of a mentally retarded son, but we still learned and grew immensely through the process of caring for him. In hindsight, I can see that before Matthew came into my life I was an impatient, selfish person in many ways. But because we had Matthew, I had the opportunity to develop patience.

Waiting three or four years for your child to learn to walk and waiting even longer for him to develop other skills will help you develop patience. We also had to be sensitive to a boy who couldn't verbally communicate his needs, desires, or hurts.

Joyce and I both grew and changed through this process. We've gone through periods of hurt, frustration, and sorrow. But we also rejoiced and learned to thank God for the tiny steps of progress that most people would take completely for granted. The meaning of the name *Matthew*—"gift from God"—has become very real to us.

Joyce and I could very easily have chosen to be bitter over our son's condition. We could have let it become a source of estrangement from one another, and we could have allowed it to hinder our growth as individuals. But God enabled us to select the path of acceptance. We have grown and matured—*together*. Not instantly, but over the course of several years.

Matthew became the refining agent that God used to change us.

A Story of Preparation

Through Matthew, my wife and I discovered a great deal about the way God works—in particular, how He prepares us for what He has in store for us. In time, we realized that He had prepared us years ahead for Matthew's birth, though we didn't realize the preparation had been taking place until we knew of his condition.

Here's how He did it:

When I was in seminary I was required to write a thesis. Not knowing what to write about, I asked one of my professors to suggest a topic. She assigned me the topic "The Christian Education of the Mentally Retarded Child." I knew absolutely nothing about the subject, but I learned in a hurry. I read books, went to classes, observed training sessions in hospitals and homes, and finally wrote the thesis. I rewrote it twice, and my wife typed it twice before it was accepted.

Later on, as part of my graduate studies in psychology, I was required to serve several hundred hours of internship in a school district, which assigned me the task of testing mentally retarded children and placing them in their respective classes. Also, while I was serving as minister of education in a church, the church board asked me to develop a Sunday school program for retarded children. My duties included developing the ministry and the curriculum and training the teachers.

One evening, before Matthew was born, Joyce and I were talking, and one of us (I can't remember which one) observed, "Isn't it interesting that we have all this exposure to retarded children? We've been learning so much. Could it be that God is preparing us for something that is going to occur later in our lives?"

Within a year, Matthew was born, and eight months after that his seizures began. The uncertainty we had felt over the rate of his progress became a deep concern. When we finally learned the full truth, we began to see how the Lord had prepared us for Matthew and for becoming Marriage Keepers.

Where does the call to suffering enter into this whole process? Romans 8:16–17 says, "The Spirit himself testifies with our spirit that we are God's children. Now if we are children, then we are heirs—heirs of God and co-heirs with Christ, if indeed we share in his sufferings in order that we may also share in his glory."

In the minor or major crises that will undoubtedly occur in life in general and in marriage in particular, each person will experience some hurt. But when we as married couples learn to share that hurt, it diminishes. But it also becomes part of our marital stories.

Lewis B. Smedes describes marital suffering in this way:

> Anybody's marriage is a harvest of suffering. Romantic lotus-eaters may tell you marriage was designed to be a pleasure-dome for erotic spirits to frolic in self-fulfilling relations. But they play you false. Your marriage vow was a promise to suffer. Yes, to suffer; I will not take it back.... You *promised* to suffer *with*. It made sense, because the person you married was likely to get hurt along the route, sooner or later, more or less, but hurt he or she was bound to get. And you promised to hurt *with* your spouse. A marriage is a life of shared pain.[3]

You have a story—tell it. Tell it again and again.

For Your Consideration

1. In what area of your life and marriage do you most need to apply James 1:2–3?

2. There are a number of questions in the first few pages of this chapter. As a couple, return to them and enjoy your discussion together.

3. Take time to construct the story of your marriage. Who would benefit from hearing it?

Recommended Resources

Quiet Times for Couples: A Daily Devotional, H. Norman Wright (Harvest House).

After You Say "I Do" Devotional: Meditations for Every Couple, H. Norman Wright (Harvest House).

Chapter Ten

WHAT'S MISSING?

THE FOLLOWING IS the kind of thing I hear often from husbands and wives who come to me because they feel that something "isn't quite right" in their marriage:

> Something's missing. I'm not sure what it is. We connect. We get along. We're both satisfied. We interact well with our minds. We're in tune emotionally. We're both able to play together. And our physical relationship is good. But every now and then I wonder...are we missing something? Is there something more?

Perhaps you've been there. Maybe that's where you're at right now. You have a feeling—a constant gnawing feeling or one that comes and goes—that something is missing from your marriage, but you can't quite put your finger on what it is.

Sometimes it's obvious to us what is missing from our marriages. We become so familiar with the person we're married to and how we get along that if one thing is amiss, we know immediately what it is.

It's very much like when I take a bite of my favorite chocolate/coffee-flavored cake and realize that one ingredient has been left out. It's easy to figure out what is missing from the cake because I am used to it tasting a certain way, so I can compare. On the other hand, if I'd never eaten this cake before and one day took a bite, I wouldn't be able to tell if something was missing at all.

I've talked to many who never knew what was missing in their marriage. They were satisfied with what they had and didn't realize there could be more…much more.

Sometimes it's simply a matter of not being, as Genesis 2:24 puts it, "one flesh."

Truly Being "One Flesh"

When we read what the Bible says about those who are married being "one flesh," most of us think first of the married couple coming together physically and becoming one. But this idea of being "one flesh" has many facets to it.

Couples become one in their minds as they share their thoughts and beliefs. There is a discovery process as this area of the relationship unfolds. It's an ongoing learning experience.

In books and in marriage seminars, the idea of "emotional oneness" for married couples has been given a lot of attention over the past few decades. It is now seen as the glue that makes oneness in marriage possible. Sadly, in some marriages only one partner is invested emotionally, and this puts the marriage in the "at risk" category.

Another facet of being one flesh in a marriage—one that is vitally important—is spiritual oneness. For many, this is just a term for something that is in some ways the most difficult part of marriage—simply because it involves the greatest vulnerability. Spiritual oneness, however, is at the very core of God's script for marriage.

One husband said:

When it came to the day-to-day sharing of our own scriptural journey, it wasn't there. Privacy was the rule.

Jan would want us to read something together and I would be too busy. She would want us to pray and I would be too tired.

She would share something deeply personal, but I would not respond. I would listen intently, but my sympathetic stares were followed with deafening silence. On the rare occasions when I did respond it was only with a summarization of what she had said, in acknowledgment, but never a personal reflection.

To Jan, my avoidant behavior communicated that I was not interested in spiritual matters and to some extent that I did not care about her needs. Gradually my excuses and my silence took their toll and she tired of her efforts. The requests for my involvement, the statements of her need, the times of her own personal sharing—all of these tapered off. Jan seemed to resign herself to the fact that it just was not going to happen.[1]

The transparency involved in spiritual oneness is a huge barrier for some married couples, mostly because it's so emotionally risky. But it's worth every ounce of effort because it's the true bonding and substance of a marriage. And it's part of Marriage Keeping, too.

There are many different expressions for spiritual oneness, or "marriage spirituality" as I sometimes call it. For some, it shows itself through theological discussions and study. For others, it's the mentoring and teaching of other couples in how to study and pray for one another that makes the couple more connected. Still others are drawn closer by sitting and listening to the hymns of faith, then talking about what they mean and when they first heard them. For most, spiritual oneness finds as an expression the intimate experience of regularly praying together as a couple.

Marriage spirituality is the coming together of a couple for the purpose of learning how to relate to God together and to experience Him at work in their lives in similar as well as unique ways. It's allowing the new life in Christ to be in every area and arena of their life together. It's a heart's desire to be close to God and submit to His direction for their lives. It's the willingness to seek His guidance together and to allow the teaching of His Word in their everyday lives.

It's also a willingness to allow God to help them overcome their sense of discomfort over sharing spiritually and begin to see marriage as a spiritual adventure. It's sharing the story of their individual spiritual journeys with one another.

The following are questions couples can read and answer together in order to help them share their spiritual adventure:

- What did your parents believe about God, Jesus, church, prayer, and the Bible?
- What was your definition of being spiritually alive?
- Which parent did you see as being spiritually alive?
- What specifically did each of your parents teach you directly and indirectly about spiritual matters?
- Where did you first learn about God? about Jesus? about the Holy Spirit? At what age?
- What was your *best* experience in church as a child? as a teen?
- What was your *worst* experience in church as a child? as a teen?
- Describe your conversion experience. When and where did it happen? Who else was involved?
- Describe your baptism. What did it mean to you?
- Which Sunday school teacher influenced you the most? In what way?
- Which minister influenced you the most? In what way?
- What questions did you have as a child/teen about your faith? Who gave you answers?
- Did an experience at camp or some other special meeting affect you spiritually?
- Did you read the Bible as a teen?
- Did you memorize Scripture as a child or teen? Do you remember any now?

- As a child, if you could have asked God any questions, what would they have been?
- As a teen, if you could have asked God any questions, what would they have been?
- If you could ask God any questions now, what would they be?
- What would have helped you in growing more spiritually when you were growing up?
- Did anyone disappoint you spiritually as a child? If so, how has that affected you as an adult?
- When you went through difficult times as a child or teen, how did that affect your faith?
- What has been the greatest spiritual experience of your life?

Marriage spirituality means going to prayer about things you never would have thought of praying about together. What everyday or even mundane issues do you need to pray about together?

Howard Hendricks shared:

We can gather all the facts needed in making a decision. We can thrash out our differences as to the shape and direction our decision should take. We can put off the decision while we allow the relevant information to simmer in our minds. Even then, however, we may be uneasy: We still don't know what is best to do, and the right decision just won't come.

When we turn to the Lord Jesus Christ and open

our consciences to His Spirit's leading, some new events, remembrances and forgotten facts will come to us. A whole new pattern will emerge. We can then move with abandon in a whole new direction that we had not previously considered. Looking back, we may conclude that God's providence delivered us from what would have been the worst possible decision. Jesus as Lord made the difference between deliverance and destruction.[2]

There's No "I" in "We"

Marriage spirituality is part of a new "we" emphasis in the relationship. It's a shared experience above and beyond the individual spiritual journey. It's not just what you read, or what or how you pray. It's about making life decisions concerning lifestyle, career, relationships, and resources in light of your shared faith. It's bringing everything to the foot of the cross.

Marriage spirituality will give meaning to the events of the life of a couple. I've sat with both spiritually connected and spiritually disconnected couples during their time of trauma. Those who were spiritually connected were able to grieve together and grow together, even though their styles of grieving were different from one another. Those who maintained their individual spirituality—though they were joined together in marriage—grieved separately and had difficulty moving closer. Some of these marriages didn't make it.

Couples who are enduring difficulty can hear God speaking to them and working through them when they are spiritually joined. They can bond more deeply as they weep together, pray together, and apply God's Word together. These are those who not only survive but grow—as a couple and as individuals. A shared spirituality in marriage means that both the husband and the wife grow individually in the spiritual sense, rather than one carrying the other.

We need God to be at the center of every dimension of our marriages. Unfortunately, some couples tend to pull away from God rather than draw near to Him when difficulties arise. We need to remember that during times of difficulty—when it seems that God is distant from us—that God hasn't gone anywhere. All we need to do is reach out to Him in prayer—together and individually.

How to Pray Together

A lot of couples who are new at marriage spirituality struggle with how to pray together. I always suggest that they start by praying *for* one another. I tell them to try praying for their spouse daily, whenever he or she comes to mind, asking God to lead and bless him or her.

Some couples take that another step and call one another daily to say that they're praying for one another and to ask what they can pray about. Other couples, as they prepare to part for the day, ask one another, "How can I best pray for you today?" My wife came up with a creative way to let me know she was praying for me: When I'm traveling I often find notes she has left in my clothes telling me that she's praying for me.

The easiest way to actually begin praying *together* is to take the time and set a time to do it. For many couples, busy schedules make this difficult, but with the right commitment to doing it, it can be done. Creativity and flexibility can make it happen. It's a matter of choice.

Praying together doesn't mean taking hours at a time. Couples can embrace and pray with one another for thirty seconds before they leave for work, after dinner, or any other time they can steal a few moments. Couples can also pray together over the phone or send their prayers via e-mail or text message. They can also pray together on their cell phones as they are driving.

When you and your spouse begin praying together at home, it may be best to share some requests then pray silently together. You can also pray your fears, doubts, and hesitations. That allows both of you to "clear the air" while at the same time allowing God to work in the area you're praying about.

Friends of mine wrote the following prayers and found them to be good starting places for praying together:

> *Dear heavenly Father, we know how important*
> *it is to build a relationship with You through prayer,*
> *but we have hesitation about praying together. It seems*
> *so scary to both of us. It seems that when one of us is*
> *willing to talk about it, the other resists. Or if we do*
> *talk about it, all kinds of things come up that take our*
> *focus away from the subject of prayer. Will you help us*
> *through the maze of our lives so that we might be able*
> *to set aside just a few minutes to talk about prayer?*
> *In the name of Jesus, amen.*

Dear Father in heaven, this prayer is very new to us.
We hardly know how to pray by ourselves, let alone how
to pray as a couple. So we ask You to help us not be
intimidated by each other and to give us the courage to
come into Your presence as a couple. Together, we want
to begin to build a strong, intimate relationship with
You. We thank You in advance for Your help.
In the name of Jesus we ask this, amen.[3]

Perhaps these prayers reflect where you're at right now. If so, they may help you get a start on praying together.

Praying aloud is something most people must grow into, and it may take you a while to become comfortable doing it. Sometimes couples struggle with audible prayer because they don't communicate as well as they should in other ways. At other times, one of the spouses is intimidated from praying out loud because he or she believes that the other is more articulate and fluent. I've always thought that Joyce's prayers were much more detailed and in-depth than mine, but this has never hindered me from praying aloud. It shouldn't hinder you, either.

The Benefits of Praying Together

What does praying together do for your marriage? Listen to what three husbands had to say about it:

As a couple, we share spiritual intimacy by praying together as a family at night. We pray for one another in the morning (we try to do it often, but sometimes

ONE MARRIAGE UNDER GOD

fall away from this good habit) by asking one another, "What can I pray about for you today?" Also, we share spiritual experiences together. We participate in a couples' weekend (which is a retreat type weekend in which an encounter with Christ occurs—for each person in a different way), retreats, family camp at Forest Home each year, and conferences; and we share intimate experiences and insights that have brought about spiritual growth. Occasionally, we will share verses or readings that brought personal spiritual meaning. These all have brought us closer in our spiritual intimacy in our marriage. And though we have marital problems in other areas, our spiritual intimacy is growing. Because we desire as individuals to grow spiritually, we will endeavor to grow in our spiritual intimacy as a couple.

Another husband said:

Without a relationship with God I don't see how we would have made it through some rough times! Before we got married, I believed very strongly that my future wife knew God also. This was key to me, because when the impasses came, I knew that the same Spirit that was at work in me was at work in her. If I would respond positively to God and she would also, I knew we would make it. Many times the only thing that I could do to keep from self-destruction or blasting her away was to pray. I would either get away by myself or invite her to join me as I led us in prayer. I believe the focus on God and the mutual faith have pulled us to Him, and to each other. It is fair to say, I don't know where I would be without God!

The last husband said:

The impact of spiritual intimacy on our marriage has been quite profound. We have found that we argue much less often, and our temperaments have both been brought dramatically under the lordship of Christ over the past several years. We find great satisfaction in watching God move mightily in each other. Our communication has improved dramatically. We share at a more intimate level than at any time in our marriage. My wife is able to share with me without the previous feeling of inadequacy, and I am more attentive to her needs. The most significant improvement has been the discovery that our physical intimacy is intricately bound to our spiritual intimacy. I had never understood this concept until I experienced it, and it is still a profound mystery. The Scriptures describe the coming together as one flesh, and I never quite understood the extent to which two people truly become one. There is something marvelous that happens at the spiritual level during worship when we intertwine our own spirits with the Holy Spirit. My wife and I have found that our most intimate physical encounters have followed our most intimate spiritual worship. When I found myself irresistibly drawn to her during and after worship together, I initially felt guilt for having such strong physical desires. I had thought that the two experiences must be mutually exclusive, as though the spiritual had nothing to do with our physical relationship. After we realized that God was Himself uniting us even more intensely during our times with Him, we found a wonderful freedom to experience a physical intimacy together after worship. Rather than exclude the Lord from our intimacy, He was actually teaching us how to be more loving, attentive, energetic, and serving with each other.

There is no better marriage than one in which the man and the woman have become one not just physically and emotionally, but spiritually too. What steps will you begin taking to make that a reality in your marriage?

For Your Consideration

1. In what way would you like to develop the spiritual connection of your marriage?
2. Describe what you will do this week to draw closer together spiritually.

Recommended Reading

When Couples Pray Together, Dave and Jan Stoop (Regal Books, 2000).

The Power of a Praying Wife, Stormie Omartian (Harvest House, 1997).

The Power of a Praying Husband, Stormie Omartian (Harvest House, 2001).

SOME
CONCLUDING
THOUGHTS

THINK BACK TO your wedding day for a moment. What if someone had offered you a look into a crystal ball that would give you a preview of the next fifty years of your marriage— would you have responded with delight or disdain at that offer?

If we could see into the future of our marriages, we might make some midcourse corrections in order to avoid some of the common marital bumps and disruptions. On the other hand, it might not be good to have some of the more unpleasant experiences hanging over our heads. What's going to happen is going to happen anyway, so what's the point in worrying about it?

But do you have any control over your marital future? Somewhat. You do have some control in that the positives you build according to the script today will give you stability years from now. But you will still live with the unknown, which is a positive because it gives you the opportunity to live a life of faith and dependence upon God. There are any number of "unforeseens" that could test the mettle of your marriage, but when you allow the Lord to be at the center of your relationship, you needn't live in fear of any of them.

I don't believe it's far off to say that most people who marry do so with the hope that their marriage will last for at least fifty years. Did I think that way when I married? Probably. If nothing else, I subtly assumed it.

Remember the story of Dale and Sherry in chapter 3? I'm sure they assumed their marriage would last for decades. Three and a half years is way too short a time for them, even though they both called it a three-and-a-half-year honeymoon. What they had together in that short amount of time many couples don't get to enjoy over a full lifetime together. They made their marriage come alive and stay alive. I know it. I saw it.

In the months following Sherry's death, Dale and I talked often and extensively about the grief he experienced. One day we talked about how we believed that God would someday use his experience of losing a wife to cancer to help another man in a similar circumstance. That is what Scripture tells us God often does with our hurts: "Praise be to the God and Father of our Lord Jesus Christ, the Father of compassion and the God of all comfort, who comforts us in all our troubles, so that we can comfort those in any trouble with the comfort we ourselves have received from God" (2 Corinthians 1:3–4).

Little did either of us know the first husband Dale would help would be me.

In October of 2003, a dark cloud crept over the horizon and darkened the skies above Joyce and me and our forty-four-year marriage. The darkness didn't just linger for a while and then move on, either. On the contrary, it stayed and then intensified.

This dark cloud had a name—brain cancer. Inoperable and

probably stage-three brain cancer. This took us completely by surprise. As Joyce commented one morning, "But these things happen to *other* people." (She then added, "There's another title for one of your books.")

It's not that we hadn't endured crises before in our marriage. Like most couples, we'd had our share. Early in our marriage, Joyce went through a physical illness. She recovered and we began to grow individually and as a couple as a result. A few years later—in between our two children—came a miscarriage. After that came Matthew, our special son. We traveled the path of keeping our special-needs son at home for eleven years.

We learned to live with continual losses while still enjoying a fairly normal lifestyle. The small losses eventually turned into a major one when Matthew finally died, which was the beginning of a journey through grief.

I don't know that we ever thought, *We've had our life experiences; we don't need any more.* But when we received the news of Joyce's malignant brain tumor, it was as though life began moving in slow motion.

We all know that these things happen to people, but we never expect them to happen to us. When they *do* happen, we feel singled out and picked on. It's as though someone has said, "Tag, you're it!" and we didn't want to play this game in the first place.

When a sudden and shocking event invades and disrupts our lives, we tend to think that it's so strange and out of the ordinary. But Peter tells us, "Beloved, think it not strange concerning the fiery trial which is to try you, as though some strange thing happened unto you" (1 Peter 4:12, KJV). *The*

Message translation puts this even stronger: "Friends, when life gets really difficult, don't jump to the conclusion that God isn't on the job. Instead, be glad that you are in the very thick of what Christ experienced. This is a spiritual refining process, with glory just around the corner" (vv. 12–13).

Perhaps the way I felt is best described by the title of a book by Dr. David Jeremiah, *A Bend in the Road*. But it was more than a bend; it was like our own personal ground zero. Mike Macintosh wrote about personal ground zeros in his book *When Your World Falls Apart*:

> All of us experience ground zeros in our lives, great losses that shake our foundations, our lives, our faith—loss of career, loved ones, marriages, children, grandchildren— times in our lives where we are overwhelmed by tragedy or just the sheer magnitude of events, when we feel helpless and it seems that the great towers of our lives are about to crumble into a heap of ruin, crushing us beneath them…. Ground zero events are watersheds in the lives of God's people. They can either *make* or *break* a life.[1]

We like to think of life as predictable, but that is an illusion and wishful thinking. Each day goes by too fast as well as too slow. It's too fast as it eats up the time we have remaining…and too slow when it involves the healing process. There is no certainty, but a walk of faith has taken its place.

No one can predict when your life here will end and you'll transition into heaven. We do know that it won't be according to your timetable. Life here is limited, and I've learned to change my priorities, to hear more of what is being said, to take my wife's requests as privileges to serve and not mere chores, and to pray and share devotional thoughts more. I've learned to look for ways to be together with my wife that I might have missed before, to be thankful for and talk about all the rich experiences and memories that make up my marital history, and to cherish walking around the yard looking at the sunrise.

I look at Joyce through different eyes now. I want to express my love, my concerns, my hurt, and my hopes more. We remain hopeful, and with the number of people praying for us we feel supported.

I wish there were more I could do, but I don't want to do for Joyce what she can enjoy doing for herself. So we're both in a new time of learning about life, ourselves, and our marriage. God has used every experience to mold and shape us. And we grew closer together.

Please don't wait for a crisis or an upset to make the changes I've talked about in this book. Heed my friend Dale's words: "Enjoy every moment you have together, and never take them for granted."

For an update on Joyce, please visit the website:
www.hnormanwright.com.

NOTES

Chapter 1

1. David P. Gushee, *Getting Marriage Right* (Grand Rapids, MI: Baker Books, 2004), 36.
2. William Doherty, *Take Back Your Marriage* (New York: The Guilford Press, 2001), 7.
3. Michele Werner Davis, *The Divorce Remedy* (New York: Simon & Schuster, 2001), 35.
4. Gushee, *Getting Marriage Right*, 190.
5. Alice P. Mathews and M. Gay Hubbard, *Marriage Made in Eden* (Grand Rapids, MI: Baker Books, 2004), 243.
6. Ibid., 246.

Chapter 2

1. Gary Thomas, *Sacred Marriage* (Grand Rapids, MI: Zondervan, 2000), 33.
2. Ibid., 13.
3. Ibid., 36.
4. Dan Allender and Tramper Longman, *Intimate Allies* (Wheaton, IL: Tyndale, 1995), 20–21.
5. Jim Smoke, *Facing 50* (Nashville, TN: Thomas Nelson, 1994), 40–41.
6. Allender and Longman, *Intimate Allies*, 25–30.
7. Ibid., 30–34.
8. Ibid., 275.

9. Ed Young, *The 10 Commandments of Marriage* (Chicago: Moody Publishing, 2003), 11.
10. Gregory K. Popcak, *The Exceptional Seven Percent* (New York: Citadel Press, 2000), 40.
11. Ibid., 73.

Chapter 3

1. Sharyn Wolf, *How to Stay Lovers for Life* (New York: Dutton, 1997), 18.
2. Dwight Small, *After You've Said I Do* (Westwood, NJ: Revell, 1968), 22.
3. Phillip C. McGraw, PhD, *Relationship Rescue* (New York: Hyperion, 2000), 261.
4. Don Harvey, *The Drifting Marriage* (Grand Rapids, MI: Revell, 1988), 44.
5. Gary Chapman, *Covenant Marriage* (Nashville, TN: Broadman and Holman, 2003), 29.

Chapter 4

1. Bryan Chapell, *Each for the Other* (Grand Rapids, MI: Baker Books, 1998), 32.
2. Ibid., 47–50.
3. Ibid., 51.
4. Ibid., 52.
5. Thomas H. Maugh II, "Study's Advice to Husbands: Accept Wife's Influence" *Los Angeles Times*, A1, Feb. 22, 1998.
6. Chapell, *Each for the Other*, 81.
7. Ibid., 113.
8. Dr. Emerson Eggerichs, *Love and Respect* (Nashville, TN: Integrity, 2004), 37.
9. From a Focus on the Family broadcast with E. V. Hill, on the death of his wife, February 1995.

Chapter 5

1. Thornton Wilder, *3 Plays,* selection from "The Skin of Our Teeth" (New York: Perennial, 1998), 200–1.
2. Rebecca Cutter, *When Opposites Attract* (New York: Dutton, 1994), 189.
3. Ibid., 196–97.
4. Harvey, *The Drifting Marriage*, 215.
5. Stephen R. Covey, *First Things First* (1996), quoted in Scott Stanley, *The Heart of Commitment* (Nashville, TN: Thomas Nelson, 1998), 36–39.
6. Ibid., 27.

Chapter 6

1. *U.S. Bureau of Census: Marital Status and Living Together*, March 1997, Bureau Population Reports Series, p. 20, No. 506, Washington DC: 1998.
2. David Gudgel, *Before You Live Together* (Ventura, CA: Regal Books, 2004), 30–31.
3. Ibid., 34–35.
4. Judith S. Wallenstein and Sandra Blakeslee, *The Good Marriage* (New York: Houghton Mifflin, 1995), 117–78. Also, Alan Booth and David Johnson, "Premarital Cohabitation and Marital Success," *Journal of Family Issues* (1988), 261–70. Also, T. R. Bafakrishnan, et al., "A Hazard Model of the Corvariates of Marriage Dissolution in Canada," *Demography*, vol.24 (1987), 295–406. Also, Neil Bennett, Ann Klimas Blanc, and David E. Bloom, "Commitment and the Modern Union: Assessing the Link Between Cohabitation and Subsequent Marital Instability," *American Sociological Review*, vol. 53 (1988): 127–38. Also, James A. Sweet and Larry L. Bumpass, "Waves 1 and 2: Data Description and Documentation," *A National Survey of Families and Households*, February 13, 2003. http://www.ssc.wisc.edu/nsfh/home/htr (accessed March 31,

2003). Also, Scott M. Stanley and Howard Markman, *Marriage in the '90s: A Nationwide Random Phone Survey* (Denver, CO: Prep. 1997). Also, David Whitman, "The Trouble with Premarital Sex," *U.S. News and World Report* (May 19, 1997), 57–64. Also, David R. Hall and John Z. Zhao, "Cohabitation and Divorce in Canada," *Journal of Marriage and the Family* (May 1995), 421–27. Also, Glenn T. Stanton, *Why Marriage Matters* (Colorado Springs, CO: Pinon, 1997), 57–59.

5. Gudgel, *Before You Live Together,* 39–40.
6. Chuck Colson, "Trial Marriages on Trial. Why They Don't Work," *Breakpoint* (March 20, 1995). Also, Jan E. Stets and Murray A. Straus, "The Marriage License as a Hitting License: A Comparison of Assaults in Dating, Cohabitating and Married Couples," *Journals of Family Violence*, vol. 41 (1989): 39. Also, "Bureau of Justice Statistics," *U.S. Department of Justice.* http://www.ojp.usdoj.gov/bjs/abstract/cv73.95htm (accessed April 4, 2003).
7. Gudgel, *Before You Live Together*, 45.
8. Larry L. Bompass and James A. Sweet, "National Estimates of Collaboration," *Demography,* vol. 26 (1989): 6115–25. Also, Lynne N. Casper and Suzanne M. Branchi, *Continuity and Change in the American Family* (Thousand Oaks, CA: Sage Publications, 2002). Also, Larry L. Bompass, "National Survey of Families and Households Working Papers," nos. 2 and 5, collected by the Center for Demography and Ecology, University of Wisconsin, 1989.
9. Gudgel, *Before You Live Together*, 32.
10. Linda J. Waite and Maggie Gallagher, *The Case for Marriage* (New York: Doubleday, 2000), 46.

Chapter 7

1. Judith S. Wallenstein, Julia M. Lewis, and Sandra Blakeslee, *The Unexpected Legacy of Divorce: The 25 Year Landmark Study* (New York: Hyperion, 2000), xxxiii, 298–99.

2. Edward Teyber, *Helping Children Cope with Divorce* (San Francisco: Josey Bass, 2001), 109.

3. Jonathan Sandoval, ed., *Handbook of Crisis Counseling, Intervention, and Prevention in the Schools* (Mahwah, NJ: Lawrence Erilbaum Associates, 2001), 91.

4. Waite and Gallagher, *The Case for Marriage,* 125.

5. Stanton, *Why Marriage Matters,* 141.

6. Jane Mauldin, "The Effects of Marital Disruption on Children's Health," *Demography* 27 (1990): 431–46.

7. Jane S. Tucker, Howard S. Friedman, Joseph E. Schwartz, Michael H. Criqui, et al., "Parental Divorce: Effects on Individual Behavior and Longevity," *Journal of Personality and Social Psychology* 73 (1997): 381–91.

8. Stanton, *Why Marriage Matters,* 141.

9. Ron Deal, *The Smart Step-Family* (Minneapolis, MN: Bethany House, 2003), 107, 110.

10. "Shuttle Diplomacy," *Psychology Today* (July/August 1993): 15–16.

11. William Doherty, *Take Back Your Marriage* (New York: The Guildford Press, 2001), 159–60.

Chapter 8

1. Waite and Gallagher, *The Case for Marriage*, 3.

2. Glenn T. Stanton, *Why Marriage Matters* (Colorado Springs, CO: Pinon, 1997), 80.

3. J. M. Mossey and E. Shapiro, "Self-Rated Health: A Predictor of Mortality Among the Elderly," *American Journal of Public Health*, 72 (1982): 800–8.

4. Waite and Gallagher, *The Case for Marriage*, 49.

5. Ibid., 50.

6. Ibid., 47–51.

7. Ibid., 54–56.

8. Ibid., 66–71.

9. Ibid., 96.

10. Ibid., 104.

11. Ibid., 112.

12. Joseph Lupton and James P. Smith, "Marriage Assets and Savings," in *Marriage and the Economy,* Shohana Grassland-Schechtman, ed., (Cambridge, England: Cambridge University Press).

13. Waite and Gallagher, *The Case for Marriage*, 115–16.

Chapter 9

1. Jerry Jenkins, *Loving Your Marriage Enough to Protect It* (Brentwood, TN: Wolgemuth and Hyatt, 1989), 142.

2. Doherty, *Take Back Your Marriage,* 134.

3. Lewis B. Smedes, *How Can It Be All Right When Everything Is All Wrong?* (San Francisco: Harper & Row, 1982), 61.

Chapter 10

1. Donald R. Harvey, *The Spiritually Intimate Marriage* (Grand Rapids, MI: Fleming H. Revell, 1991), 24.

2. Howard and Jeanne Hendricks, eds., with LaVonne Neff, *Husbands and Wives*, from an article by Wayne Oates (Wheaton, IL: Victor Books, 1988), 158.

3. Dave and Jan Stoop, *When Couples Pray Together* (Ventura, CA: Regal Books, 2000), 36–37.

Some Concluding Thoughts

1. Mike Macintosh, *When Your World Falls Apart: Life Lessons from a Ground Zero Chaplain* (Colorado Springs, CO: Cook Communications, 2002), 23.